WONDER CITY OF THE WORLD

NEW YORK CITY

TRAVEL POSTERS

WONDER CITY OF THE WORLD
NEW YORK CITY
TRAVEL POSTERS

By Nicholas D. Lowry

With Angelina Lippert, Tim Medland, and Catherine Bindman

Additional essays by Colette Gaiter, Jon Key, Jennifer Rittner, and Michele Washington

CERNUNNOS

TABLE OF CONTENTS

INTRODUCTION

BY ANGELINA LIPPERT
CHIEF CURATOR & DIRECTOR
OF CONTENT OF POSTER HOUSE

The greatest advertisement for New York City was a gift from France, the country most associated with the dawn of the poster. While not in traditional paper form, this ad was subsequently adorned, in 1885, with the founding ethos of the city:

Not like the brazen giant of Greek fame,
With conquering limbs astride from land to land;
Here at our sea-washed, sunset gates shall stand
A mighty woman with a torch, whose flame
Is the imprisoned lightning, and her name
Mother of Exiles. From her beacon-hand
Glows world-wide welcome; her mild eyes command
The air-bridged harbor that twin cities frame.
"Keep, ancient lands, your storied pomp!" cries she
With silent lips. "Give me your tired, your poor,
Your huddled masses yearning to breathe free,
The wretched refuse of your teeming shore.
Send these, the homeless, tempest-tost to me,
I lift my lamp beside the golden door!"

This advertisement, this invitation, is rejecting the history and pageantry of Europe. This is not a place for nobility or first-born sons. This is a place for rebirth, for second chances, for only chances, for last-ditch efforts, for everyone that does not yet belong. It is dirty, it is hungry, and it is rough—but it welcomes you.

No other city promotes itself quite like that—and that's what made and makes New York so impossible to replicate. Over the years, it has been known by endless names, from Wonder City of the World to the far more familiar Big Apple, City of Dreams, and City That Never Sleeps. What are these nicknames trying to express but the seemingly endless promise and possibility of New York City? In the land of opportunity, it was and is the greatest frontier to conquer. From robber barons to rising stars, New York is where they proved their worth—if you can make it here, you really can make it anywhere.

Unlike other cities that have an identity tied to a historic past, New York is constantly reinventing itself. Like the myriad brands in this book that update their logos and taglines every decade, New York is always shifting, growing, and changing with each new resident. While skylines in most cities remain relatively constant, New York's manages to be both iconic and ever-evolving, equally home to the Empire State Building and the new matchsticks dotting Midtown—and in another decade, no doubt taller, more impressive structures will emerge. New York may no longer have the tallest buildings in the world, but when people think of skyscrapers, they almost undoubtedly think of Manhattan.

This book and its corresponding exhibition aim to tell the story of how advertising helped establish New York City as the unofficial capital of the world. As the most public of all forms of graphic communication, posters have to tell a story to a mass audience in under a second in order to be effective. They cannot be too specialized or too bland; they must strike the perfect balance of being eye-catching enough to make the viewer pause, but universal enough to appeal to everyone—and yet, so many of these posters are so different from one another. Where other cities rely on a handful of monuments or a semi-recognizable skyline, New York advertising embraces every corner of the city to entice visitors, because every inch of New York is the promise of opportunity, adventure, and escape. While many of these designs highlight obvious landmarks like the Statue of Liberty or the Twin Towers, others find that the allure of a tugboat on the East River or a ritzy dinner in a well-appointed skyscraper is enough to encapsulate the mystique of Manhattan.

In addition to acting as a history of who was being asked to come to New York City, these posters also document how the city physically evolved between the nineteenth and twenty-first centuries. Early images depict the crowded skyline of Lower Manhattan—demure in comparison to today's architectural monstrosities, but miraculous at the time. With each decade, buildings get taller, the cityscape swelling with carved concrete built in the name of industry. As more people wanted to visit New York, bigger ships were needed, resulting in piers that literally dug into the island in order to fit within the Hudson River. Soon, though, airlines would overtake ships as the primary means of transportation, the dawn of the lower-priced "tourist class" making the city even more accessible to a global audience. Be it by rail or sea, bus or plane, New York wanted the world to visit it or make it home.

These posters also bear witness to the birth of some of the city's greatest monuments: Grand Central Terminal, the first all-glass skyscraper, the Chrysler Building, the Empire State Building, and the United Nations Secretariat Building. They serve as a record of many beloved sites that no longer exist, from the original Pennsylvania Station to the Twin Towers. They present the set dressing of collective hopes and dreams of generations of immigrants and adventure-seekers, all striking out to make New York City their own.

Most importantly, though, these images serve to glorify the city. New York constantly speaks to its perceived successes, to the commercial deals struck that enriched the few but did nothing for the many, to the captains of industry who used its streets and avenues as their playgrounds. Posters rarely document those who did not make it. Instead, they capitalize on the promise that anyone can be a Rockefeller or a Robert Moses. They advertise the dream, the wonder of the city.

FOREWORD

THE WONDER CITY OF THE WORLD: MYTHMAKING AND THE METROPOLIS

BY NICHOLAS D. LOWRY

New York wasn't always a "Wonder City." For centuries, the area at the mouth of what is now New York Harbor was home to the Lenape people. In 1524, the first European explorer, Giovanni da Verrazzano, sailed into what is now New York Bay, and in 1609, almost a century later, Henry Hudson's exploration on behalf of the Dutch East India Company helped establish New Amsterdam, a Dutch-controlled settlement. With approximately 520 miles of coastline—more than Los Angeles, San Francisco, Miami, and Boston combined—New York was an important port long before it was a prominent tourist destination. Its natural, deep-water harbor and protected landings made it a desirable, accessible, and safe haven for ships. The opening of the Erie Canal in 1825 connected the Hudson River to the Great Lakes, giving merchants access to the interior of the country and making New York Harbor even more commercially attractive. By the time the Civil War began in 1861, New York was one of the three biggest ports in the world.

As the city grew, it became a hub for rail transport and sea travel; a point of entry for immigrants, merchandise, and dreams; and the commercial capital of the nation. It soon evolved into a bustling, thriving urban center. The opening of the Brooklyn Bridge in 1883 and the dedication of the Statue of Liberty in 1886 introduced two impressive landmarks that began to shape the city's modern visual identity. When, in 1898, greater New York was consolidated into a single city consisting of five boroughs, it also emerged as one of the world's largest urban areas, second only to London in terms of population. Further, from the 1870s, a series of skyscrapers slowly began to populate the skyline; the process escalated in the 1890s—when the term began to be commonly used—establishing the densest concentration of tall buildings in the world at the time. From the 1870s, too, a system of elevated trains ran throughout the city; these were fully electrified in the early 1900s, and, by 1904, a subway was running underground. It was hardly an exaggeration to call this buzzing, dramatic, unique place a "Wonder City."

The phrase, the brainchild of marketers, had appeared in newspaper and magazine advertisements and articles sporadically through the final decades of the nineteenth century in reference to many cities but mainly New York. A number of cities around the country and in Europe also used it in their promotions at the time. By 1914, the phrase appeared on a New York souvenir booklet. Such popular keepsakes, along with postcards and postcard books, spread images of the city and its nickname. Previous efforts by advertisers to sum up New York in a distinctive manner had been less successful. Phrases like the "American Cosmopolis," the "First City of the World," "City of Marvels," and the "Foremost City in the World" never really gained traction, but the fact that New York was truly a "Wonder City" was apparent to all.

New York's explosive growth from the end of the nineteenth century ultimately produced more travel posters than were designed for any other city in the world, a host of images as varied as its ever-shifting identity, showing it from the water, from the ground, and, eventually, from the air. This book tracks how New York City was represented to travelers, immigrants, and tourists over the decades. It is a visual, graphic experience, one that encourages the viewer to exult in all the ways artists captured the multitude and the magnitude of the thriving metropolis, selling the hustle and the bustle, the bright lights, and the imposing structures, sometimes representing moments of intimacy and slice-of-life imagery within the urban canyons and among the ziggurats.

EARLY NEW YORK TOURISM

Much of early American tourism, which began in the years after the War of 1812, was centered in the Hudson River Valley. The wealthy would go on a "fashionable tour," heading up toward the luxurious destinations of Saratoga Springs and Ballston Spa. By the 1820s, due to improvements in transportation, tourism was no longer an exclusively upper-class pursuit, and travel and hotels became more widely accessible. Beginning in the 1870s, Saratoga was the nation's top high-end destination due to its hot springs and casinos. During these years, tourism in New York City also flourished, and the city was the subject of multiple guidebooks and travelogs. It was not, however, promoted by illustrated posters until the final decade of the nineteenth century.

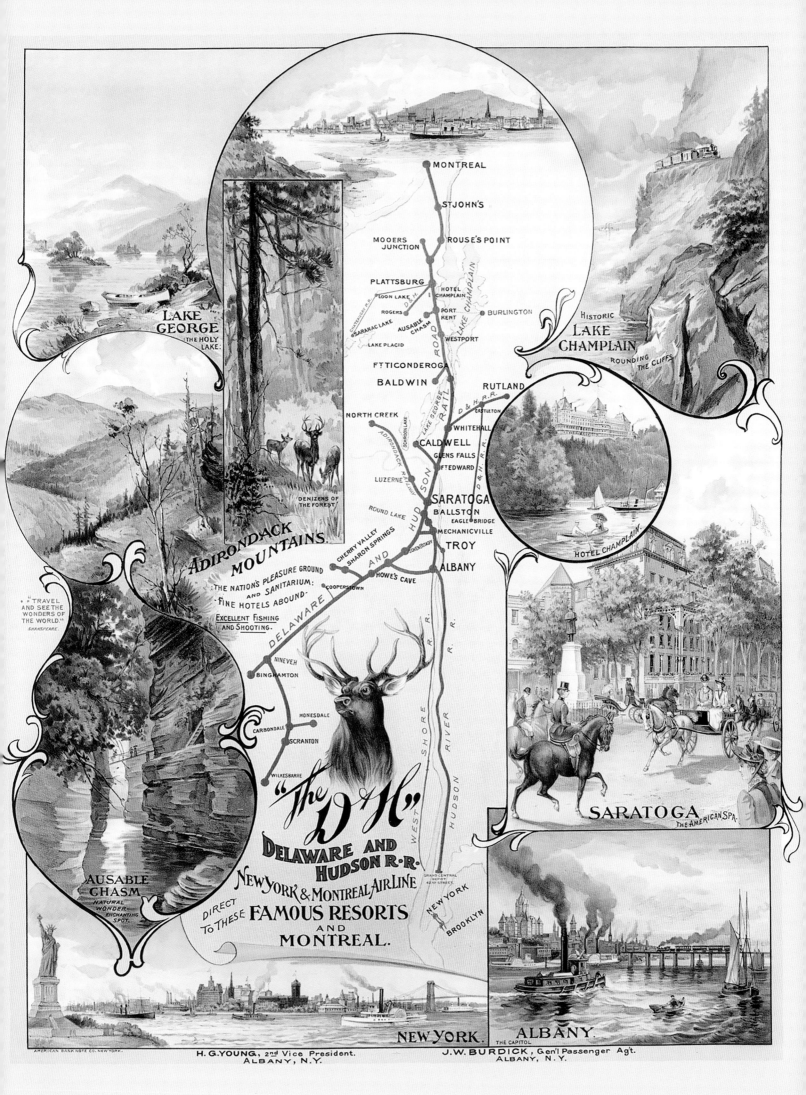

LAKE GEORGE
(THE HOLY LAKE)

DENIZENS OF THE FOREST

ADIRONDACK MOUNTAINS.
THE NATION'S PLEASURE GROUND
AND SANITARIUM:
FINE HOTELS ABOUND.
EXCELLENT FISHING
AND SHOOTING.

"TRAVEL AND SEE THE WONDERS OF THE WORLD."
SHAKSPEARE.

AUSABLE CHASM
NATURAL WONDER—ENCHANTING SPOT.

MONTREAL
ST. JOHN'S
MOOERS JUNCTION
ROUSE'S POINT
PLATTSBURG
LOON LAKE
HOTEL CHAMPLAIN
ROGERS
SARANAC LAKE
AUSABLE CHASM
PORT KENT
BURLINGTON
LAKE PLACID
WESTPORT
FT. TICONDEROGA
BALDWIN
RUTLAND
NORTH CREEK
CASTLETON
WHITEHALL
CALDWELL
GLENS FALLS
FT. EDWARD
LUZERNE
SARATOGA
ROUND LAKE
BALLSTON
EAGLE BRIDGE
CHERRY VALLEY
MECHANICVILLE
SHARON SPRINGS
SCHENECTADY
TROY
HOWE'S CAVE
ALBANY
COOPERSTOWN
DELAWARE
NINEVEH
BINGHAMTON
HONESDALE
CARBONDALE
SCRANTON
WILKESBARRE
WEST SHORE R. R.
HUDSON RIVER R. R.
GRAND CENTRAL DEPOT 42ND STREET
NEW YORK
BROOKLYN

Historic
LAKE CHAMPLAIN
ROUNDING THE CLIFFS

HOTEL CHAMPLAIN

SARATOGA
THE AMERICAN SPA.

"The D&H"
DELAWARE AND HUDSON R·R·
NEW YORK & MONTREAL AIR LINE
DIRECT TO THESE FAMOUS RESORTS
AND MONTREAL.

NEW YORK.

ALBANY.
THE CAPITOL

AMERICAN BANK NOTE CO. NEW YORK.

H. G. YOUNG, 2nd Vice President.
ALBANY, N.Y.

J. W. BURDICK, Gen'l Passenger Ag't.
ALBANY, N.Y.

13

**Cie Générale Transatlantique/
Paris–Le Havre–New-York**,
c. 1892

Designer Unknown
*Image Courtesy of Swann Auction
Galleries*

- The shipping company promoted
here was founded in 1855 by the
brothers Emile and Isaac Péreire as the
Compagnie Générale Maritime. In 1861,
its name was changed to the Compagnie
Générale Transatlantique (later known
as "C.G.T." or "French Line"), and the
brothers were subsidized by the French
government to run a steamship service
to New York. The company's Le Havre–
New York line was inaugurated in 1864.

- The poster shows French Line's SS *La
Touraine* (its name is visible on the hull
in a variant of the poster) leaving New
York and crossing the path of another
French Line ship that celebrates its
arrival by emitting smoke streams in the
national colors shared by France and
the United States. *La Touraine*, which
made its maiden journey to New York in
June 1891, was the company's fastest
ship and made the crossing from Le
Havre in under seven days.

- At left, the Statue of Liberty, a gift from
France to the United States, dedicated
in 1886, just a few years before this
poster was published, serves as a
further reminder of the special relationship between the two revolutionary

republics. The beams of light emanating
from the statue's torch illuminate the
scene and reference its original official
name: Liberty Enlightening the World.

- The Statue of Liberty's symbolic
association with New York and with the
immigrants arriving in the city's harbor
was established by Emma Lazarus's
poem "The New Colossus," which is
inscribed on a bronze panel set in the
pedestal. Shipping operations like French
Line relied largely on the business of
European immigrants to the United
States; between 1870 and 1920 alone,
nearly twelve million people arrived here,
most fleeing poverty, war, and perse-
cution. They typically traveled in the
steerage of these grand ocean liners.

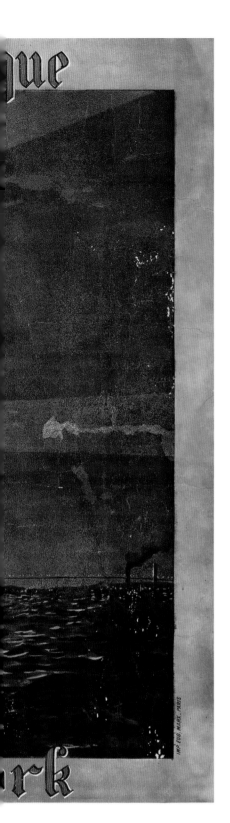

Red Star Linie / Antwerpen, 1893

Carl Saltzmann (1847–1923)
Private Collection, New York
Image Courtesy of Poster House

- This poster depicts one of Red Star Line's most famous vessels, the *Westernland*. Built in 1883, the ship was the company's first to incorporate a steel hull, two funnels, and three different classes of passenger accommodation. The Red Star Line ran regularly scheduled crossings between Belgium and the United States until 1934, when the company went bankrupt. Both Albert Einstein and Irving Berlin immigrated to the United States aboard one of its vessels.

- This advertisement was intended to encourage immigration rather than tourism to New York City. As the image predates New York's famous skyline, it incorporates the city's two most recognizable landmarks at the time: the Statue of Liberty (officially opened in October 1886) and the Brooklyn Bridge (opened in May 1883).

- Between 1873 and 1934, almost two million passengers came to the United States on the Red Star Line, the majority from Germany and Eastern Europe.

Barnum & Bailey/Coney Island,
c. 1898

Designer Unknown
*Library of Congress, Prints
& Photographs Division,
[LC-DIG-ppmsca-54817]*

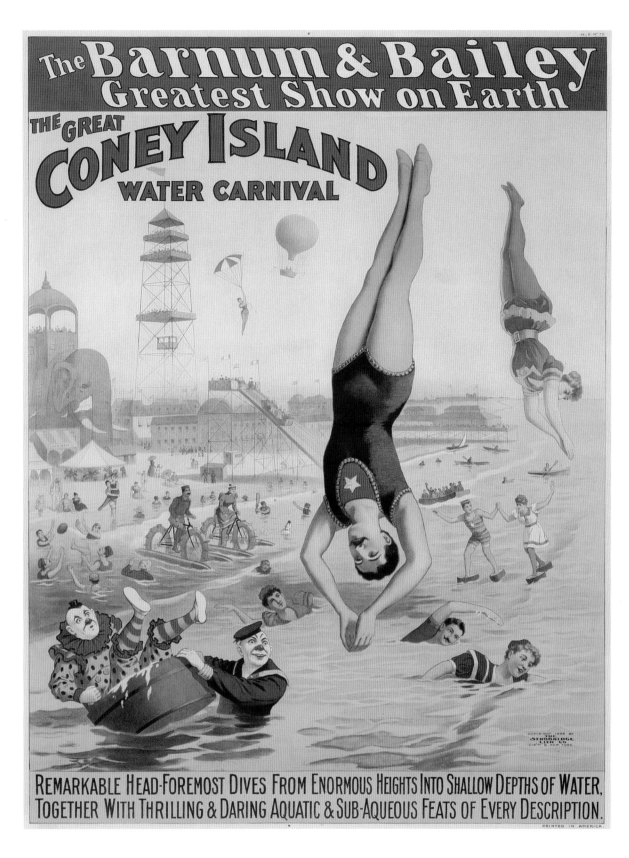

Barnum & Bailey/Coney Island, 1898

Designer Unknown
Poster Photo Archives, Posters Please, Inc., NYC

- Both of these posters were designed to promote Barnum & Bailey's "Great Coney Island Water Carnival" and combine vivid chromolithography with the boastful superlatives characteristic of much nineteenth-century advertising.

- This event, which claimed to be "a faithful reproduction of the favourite seaside resort of the residents of New York City," according to a brochure promoting a London presentation of

the spectacle, was not actually held on Coney Island. It was one of many traveling pageants, typically involving music and many costumed performers, as they reenacted scenes from various well-known stories and historical events, among them *Aladdin*, *Cinderella*, Columbus and the Discovery of America, and the life of Cleopatra.

- At the time these posters were published, Coney Island was becoming increasingly well-known across the country and beyond. Three amusement parks opened there between 1897 and 1904, and transformed the scene by charging admission, banning alcohol, and introducing a range of daring rides.

- On the far left of the first poster can be seen the Elephantine Colossus, an elephant-shaped hotel that stood on Coney Island at the corner of Surf Avenue and Twelfth Street between 1885 and 1996, when it burned down. The hotel stood twelve stories high and incorporated thirty-one rooms and a museum. In 1890, when its proprietors fell on hard times, this remarkable structure, once described as the eighth wonder of the world, was converted to a brothel.

Forepaugh & Sells Brothers/ Madison Square Garden, 1900

Designer Unknown
Poster Photo Archives, Posters Please, Inc., NYC

- During the 1870s and '80s, Adam Forepaugh and P. T. Barnum were the rival proprietors of the two largest circuses in the country. More businessman than showman (like Barnum), Forepaugh introduced such circus innovations as the first Wild West show and two tents that allowed him to separate the menagerie from the circus acts that might offend pious sensibilities. In 1900, the year this poster was produced, Forepaugh Circus, owned by then for more than a decade by James A. Bailey and James E. Cooper, merged with Sells Brothers.

- In contrast to typical circus posters depicting such attractions as trapeze artists, clowns, and exotic animals, the selling point here is the new company's "World Famous Metropolitan Home" in the grand Beaux Arts structure (with Moorish flourishes) of Madison Square Garden, completed in 1890 after designs by celebrated architect Stanford White.

- This New York landmark, later destroyed, had replaced the original building opened by William Vanderbilt on Twenty-Sixth Street and Madison Avenue in 1879 and razed a decade later when its sporting events and entertainments proved unprofitable.

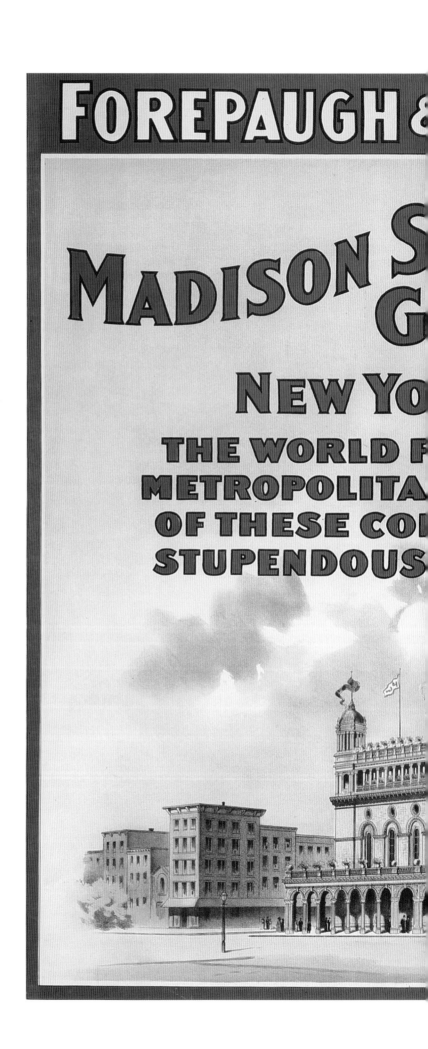

**Compagnie Générale
Transatlantique/New York/
Paris**, c. 1901

Designer Unknown
*Library of Congress, Prints
& Photographs Division,
[LC-DIG-ppmsca-58685]*

- The ship here is the SS *La Lorraine*, launched by the Compagnie Générale Transatlantique in 1900. National flags and portraits of George Washington and Lafayette, the French military officer who fought in the American Revolutionary War, and images of the company's New York and Paris locations, assert a positive alliance between the two republics.

- The building at the lower left is the CGT's New York office on lower Broadway. The image at lower right shows the Porte Monumentale (the Monumental Entrance) to the Exposition Universelle held in Paris in 1900, a world's fair intended to celebrate the cultural and technological achievements of the nineteenth century and promote those of the twentieth. The entrance, designed by René Binet, quickly became a symbol of the exposition in the international press, and would probably have been familiar to many American viewers of the poster.

- A variant of the poster shows *La Lorraine*'s sister ship, the SS *La Savoie*, which did not make its maiden journey

until 1901, when Binet's entrance had already been destroyed. Nonetheless, the recent exposition remained a potent reminder of French cultural and colonial power.

Transatlantique/
Havre-New-York, 1906

Fernand Le Quesne (1856–1932)
Image Courtesy of International Poster Gallery, Boston

- This poster almost certainly shows the SS *La Provence*, the newest of the company's ships among those listed next to the maritime objects at the lower right of the composition. The ocean liner's maiden voyage from Le Havre to New York took place in April 1906, when it was the largest ship in the French merchant marine.

- The *La Provence* could accommodate 397 first-class passengers, 205 second-class, and 900 third-class. These figures suggest that even the most luxurious ocean liners were economically dependent to some extent on modest, mostly immigrant, customers.

- As the ship sails away from New York, a woman waving a handkerchief mimics the pose of the Statue of Liberty, that great symbol of French and American unity, seen at her shoulder in the distance. Entwined French and American flags further celebrate the friendship of the two nations.

- The later history of *La Provence* was less cheerful. It was the first ship to record the distress call of the *Titanic* on the night of April 14–15, 1912, and on February 26, 1916, it was torpedoed and sunk.

NEW YORK
from GLASGOW *by the*
ANCHOR LINE

APPLY TO
THIS AGENCY.

ABOVE

New York/Anchor Line,
c. 1910

D.N.A.
Private Collection, New York
Image Courtesy of Poster House

- This poster depicts some of the most architecturally detailed renderings of Manhattan's early skyscrapers, including the Singer Building, the tallest building in the city from its completion in 1908 until the following year, when it was surpassed in height by the Metropolitan Life Tower. This sweeping southern view from the intersection of Maiden Lane and Broadway also show-cases the Washington Life Insurance Building, the Trinity and United States Realty Buildings, and the City Investing Building, all of which had been completed within the previous decade.

- Shipping companies almost always pictured one of their vessels in their travel posters. Here, Anchor Line's *Furnessia*—its only ship with a single funnel making the New York–Glasgow crossing at this time—is shown passing in front of the Statue of Liberty.

- Founded in 1855, Anchor Line was a Scottish shipping company that was ultimately acquired by Cunard in 1911. As posters published after that point typically include the Cunard name, this design had to be printed between the construction of the previously mentioned landmarks and the merger of the two companies.

- In 1968, the Singer Building became the tallest building ever to be demolished.

OPPOSITE

Cunard Line to New York,
c. 1913

Charles Pears (1873–1958)
Poster Photo Archives, Posters Please, Inc., NYC

- The design here, clearly intended to promote the Wonder City to the well-to-do tourists on the upper decks of a Cunard ocean liner, emphasizes the dazzling modernity of nighttime New York. The city is brilliantly illuminated by the lights in the many windows of its famous skyscrapers, most notably the Singer Building on lower Broadway. A vessel, presumably from the Cunard line, is dramatically silhouetted against the buildings.

- Cunard (originally called the British and North American Royal Mail Steam Packet Company) began its

transatlantic operations in July 1840, when the *Britannia* sailed to Halifax and Boston in a little over fourteen days.

- While Charles Dickens had described the Cunard steamship on which he had traveled in 1842 as "not unlike a gigantic hearse," by the time this poster was produced, the company's five passenger liners, especially the *Lusitania* and the *Mauretania*, were known for their luxury. They could also make the journey across the Atlantic in fewer than four and a half days.

- British artist Charles Pears was a dedicated yachtsman who applied his knowledge of maritime vessels to his paintings and to the posters he designed as a commercial artist for important shipping companies like Cunard and Orient. He also worked as an official naval war artist in both world wars.

T. FORMAN & SONS, NOTTINGHAM, LONDON & LIVERPOOL

CUNARD LINE
TO NEW YORK

French Line/Agenzia Fugazi,
c. 1920

Richard Rummell (1848–1924)
*Poster Photo Archives, Posters Please,
Inc., NYC*

- The poster advertises San Francisco's oldest travel agency, Agenzia Fugazi, founded in 1869 by Giovanni "John" F. Fugazi, an Italian immigrant. By 1876, the firm had become the general agent for French Line, promoted here with an image of its celebrated ship, the SS *France*. It had been refurbished and restored to commercial service in early 1920 after being requisitioned by the French navy during World War I.

- When the *France* made its maiden transatlantic journey in 1912—shortly after the sinking of the RMS *Titanic*—it was the first of a series of extremely luxurious ocean liners that would come to dominate the route in the years between the wars. In fact, this was the second of three French Line ships to be given the name, and it was also known as the Versailles of the Atlantic.

- Most of its first-class passengers were well-heeled Americans, among them diplomats, businessmen, and artistic types who appreciated the ship's Grand Siècle decor with ornate gilded furnishings in the style of the court of Sun King Louis XIV. They also enjoyed the fine dining, excellent service, and numerous entertainments, as well as such modern amenities as hot and cold water in the cabins.

- In this poster, showing the ship on its arrival in New York Harbor, three prominent skyscrapers are visible in the skyline behind: from left to right we can see the Woolworth Building (1913), at the time the tallest building in the world; the Park Row Building (1899); and the Singer Building (1908).

- The composition is based on a painting by Brooklyn-based artist Richard Rummell, who had established his illustration office on Broadway in Manhattan in the 1880s. He was known for his panoramic images, among them a series of views of American colleges.

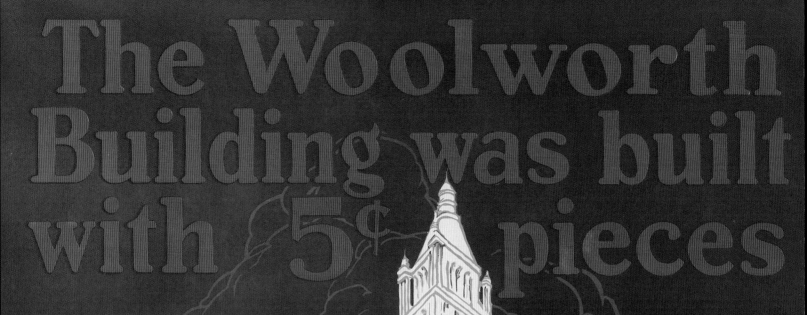

The Woolworth Building was built with 5¢ pieces

That man
who gives only
his very Best
to a 5¢ Job is
qualified to fill
a THOUSAND
DOLLAR JOB

Never Neglect the Little Things

**To Europe via America/
The "Big Ship" Route**, 1929

Frank Newbould (1887–1950)
*Image Courtesy of Swann Auction
Galleries*

- This composition, with its limited color palette and flat geometries, emphasizes the stark forms of New York's famous skyscrapers. At the far left is a partial view of the Municipal Building, completed by McKim, Mead & White in 1914, then the Woolworth Building (1913), and the New York Telephone Building (known since 2016, when it was partially converted to residential condominiums, as 100 Barclay). The Telephone Building was designed by Ralph Walker and constructed between 1923 and 1927, incorporating the highest-quality materials and the latest technologies. The grapevine motifs in the ornament of its lavishly appointed lobby are especially appropriate to a communications corporation. It was one of the city's first and most influential Art Deco skyscrapers.

- In front of the buildings, the British White Star Line's celebrated luxury ocean liner, the RMS *Olympic*, departs to the left. By the time this poster was produced, the *Olympic* was the only surviving vessel of the three luxury ships launched by White Star from 1910; the other two were the ill-fated RMS *Titanic*, sunk after hitting an iceberg in 1912, and the HMHS *Britannic*, sunk after striking a mine in 1916.

- By 1929, White Star's transatlantic operations were under pressure. While it had originally built its name on offering improved accommodations in steerage, the boom in European immigration to America after World War I had been curtailed by the Immigration Act of 1924. This further limited the rigid quotas of permitted immigrants from European countries and Great Britain; immigration from Asia was cut off altogether.

- While White Star was able to offset this to some extent by upgrading its liners for a new influx of tourists and rebranding its third class as "tourist class," it was soon affected by the Great Depression. In 1934, it merged with its rival, the Cunard Line, to create Cunard-White Star Line Ltd.

The Woolworth Building, 1925

Designer Unknown
*Image Courtesy of Swann Auction
Galleries*

- The Woolworth Building on Broadway and Park Place in Manhattan, opposite City Hall Park (represented by the line of trees at the bottom of the poster), was one of the great sights of the city. Described at its dedication in 1913 as "a cathedral of commerce," it has 60 stories and a height of 792 feet. Until 1930, when it was exceeded in height by the Chrysler Building, it was the tallest building in the world.

- It was constructed as headquarters for the company of Frank Winfield Woolworth, the American entrepreneur who had made a fortune with his famous chain of five-and-dime stores, the first of which had opened in Utica, New York, in 1879. By 1925, when this poster was published, Woolworth had stores all over the United States and was also operating in England, Germany, Canada, and Cuba. In this typical work-incentive poster, produced by Mather & Company to motivate employees in factories and offices, this success story is transformed into a moral lesson.

- Designed by Cass Gilbert, who had apprenticed with the distinguished New York architectural firm of McKim, Mead & White, this Gothic-style building constructed of masonry and terra-cotta covering a steel frame became a model for the skyscrapers that came to define the New York skyline after World War I.

EMBLEM OF A NATION

In the three decades between the dedication of the Statue of Liberty in 1886 and the entry of the United States into World War I in 1917, New York City became so prominent in the national and international imagination that it was frequently used as a visual shorthand to represent America as a whole. This is especially evident in fundraising posters produced during the war.

OPPOSITE

Food Will Win the War, 1917

Charles Edward Chambers (1883–1941)
Gift of Peter A. Blatz, Poster House
Permanent Collection
Image Courtesy of Poster House

- On May 5, 1917, Herbert Hoover was appointed head of the US Food Administration; he had already told President Woodrow Wilson that "second only to military action [food] was the dominant factor" in winning the war.

- That agency published this poster during World War I as an appeal to new immigrants to help their adopted country save wheat and other food to feed the Allies. The message—that the United States has offered them so much that now they must sacrifice something in return—is reinforced by visual reminders of the magnitude of their arrival in New York Harbor and the abundance in this new land, one they must now ration for on behalf of their new country.

- The awe-inspiring, golden skyline— perhaps playing off the old adage that the city's streets were paved with gold—would have been recognizable to and instilled pride in those who arrived from Europe by ship. Clearly visible are the Woolworth Building, the Municipal Building, and the Singer Building.

- To reach a wide range of immigrants, this poster was printed in multiple languages, including English, Yiddish, Spanish, Italian, and Hungarian.

FOOD WILL WIN THE WAR

You came here seeking Freedom
You must now help to preserve it

WHEAT is needed for the allies
Waste nothing

UNITED STATES FOOD ADMINISTRATION

War Savings Stamps, 1918

Designer Unknown
*Poster House Permanent Collection
Image Courtesy of Poster House*

- This poster shows the skyline of Lower Manhattan being protected by one of the thirty-three battleships in the United States Navy—many of which were built at the Brooklyn Navy Yard. The Singer Building, the Woolworth Building, and some of the many docks surrounding the Lower Manhattan shoreline are also depicted on either side of the vessel's lattice mast.

- War Saving Stamps were a national fundraising initiative introduced by the US government during the war that allowed citizens to invest five dollars in the war effort—a more affordable price than war bonds. Thrift stamps, valued at twenty-five cents each, could also be purchased and accumulated until the five-dollar level was achieved. Posters for the promotion of this program were displayed throughout the country during this time.

- The term "Liberty's Gateway" often referred to Ellis Island. Here, however, New York City itself is that gateway and must be protected at all costs.

IOSEPH PENNELL DEL.

THAT LIBERTY SHALL NOT PERISH FROM THE EARTH BUY LIBERTY BONDS
FOURTH LIBERTY LOAN

2-B

That Liberty Shall Not Perish from the Earth, 1918

Joseph Pennell (1857–1926)
Private Collection, New York
Image Courtesy of Poster House

- This nightmare scenario, eerily similar to the final scene in the 1968 film *Planet of the Apes*, shows New York City in flames with a squadron of German bombers overhead and a U-Boat in the bay. The Statue of Liberty is in ruins, her head lying in pieces at the water's edge, and the Brooklyn Bridge has collapsed, its cables and deck dangling into the East River.

- To raise the money needed to fight the war, Secretary of the Treasury William McAdoo proposed combining tax revenue with war-bond sales. Between the time the United States formally entered World War I on April 7, 1917, and the armistice on November 11, 1918, the country had issued five separate series of bonds, the first four of which were referred to as Liberty Bonds. The least expensive of these cost fifty dollars. The fifth and final round, known as a Victory Loan, was issued after the armistice.

- Posters for Liberty Bonds incorporated various persuasive psychological tactics, engaging viewers through fear,

patriotism, sex appeal, pride, family, democracy, and freedom. This is one of the most powerful of the dozens of different compositions created for each of the five drives.

- Originally, Joseph Pennell wanted the poster to read, "Buy Liberty Bonds or you will see this." However, the Division of Pictorial Publicity (a committee created during World War I to design propaganda posters) decided to change the title, adapting the final line of Abraham Lincoln's Gettysburg Address: "that this nation, under God, shall have a new birth of freedom—and that government of the people, by the people, for the people, shall not perish from the earth."

THE ENEMY IS AT THE GATE OF NEW YORK: JOSEPH PENNELL'S WARTIME WARNING

BY JON KEY

In 1917, author, illustrator, and printmaker Joseph Pennell noted that "when the United States wished to make public its wants, whether of men or money, it found that art—as the European countries had found—was the best medium." Shortly after America entered the World War in Europe in April of that year, the government established the Committee on Public Information with a Division of Pictorial Publicity, intended to encourage patriotism and public support for the war effort. It also provided official artists for the American Expeditionary Forces.

Joseph Pennell was among the established artists hired by the division, in addition to Howard Chandler Christy, Charles Buckles Falls, John E. Sheridan, and H. Devitt Welsh. The chairman was Charles Dana Gibson, best known for his illustrated "Gibson Girls" at the turn of the twentieth century. A caption on a photograph of a luncheon held in Washington for the division notes the presence of "the government's leading publicity men and those who are making Uncle Sam's poster. . . . Back of Mr. Hurley with gray hat, is Joseph Pennell, whose sketches have been one of the war's best contributions to art."

The creation of "Uncle Sam's" posters and images was critical to engaging the public with the government's efforts. During the previous decades, Pennell had established his professional reputation by producing illustrations that documented wartime activities, landscapes, and propaganda for governments abroad.

Born in Philadelphia on Independence Day in 1857, Joseph Pennell was raised by Quaker parents, Larkin and Rebecca Pennell, and studied under James R. Lambdin, known for his presidential portraits. After studying at the Pennsylvania Museum and School of Industrial Art and then graduating from the Pennsylvania Academy of the Fine Arts, he established his own studio in 1880, where he produced magazine illustrations. In 1884, he moved to London and worked on numerous mezzotints and lithographs, mainly of landscapes and architecture, in addition to etchings that reflect the influence of his friend and fellow American artist in London, James McNeill Whistler. While he made two sets of New York prints inspired by his visits to the city in 1904 and 1908, he did not return to live permanently in the United States until 1917.

Before the outbreak of World War I in 1914, Pennell traveled around Britain, the European continent, and the United States, documenting industrial and urban structures. In 1917, with the permission of the British government, he published a volume of his *Pictures of War Work in England*, and this was so successful that he was commissioned by the French minister of munitions to make images of the war in France. After abandoning the commission (as a Quaker, he found the front unbearably horrific), he quickly returned to the United States where his *Pictures of War Work in America* was published the following year. He also began to produce posters for the Division of Pictorial Publicity, including *Launching Another Victory Ship* and *Provide the Sinews of War*.

In *Launching Another Victory Ship*, the vast scale of the ship in comparison to that of the crowd cheering below is clearly intended to demonstrate American political might and the power of its industry. The viewer might be especially reassured by an image that shows neither Uncle Sam nor a military man but a huge metal symbol of American strength.

Pennell's *That Liberty Shall Not Perish from the Earth* (see page 33), promoting bonds for the Fourth Liberty Loan of September 1918, is the most dramatic of his wartime posters. It boldly reinforces New York's critical role in representing American democracy, as well as its capitalist and cultural innovations. It also reflects the fact that New York City had made significant efforts to assist the Allies in Europe even before America declared war on Germany in April 1917. J. P. Morgan and other New York financiers, for example, loaned $500 million to the British and French governments for goods and munitions. New York City factories also produced munitions that were shipped to Europe through New York Harbor. (This was the main embarkment point for troop and cargo ships crossing the Atlantic for Europe once the United States officially entered the war.) Soon, German-language classes ceased to be taught in the city's public schools, German works disappeared from its opera houses and concert halls, and hamburgers were temporarily renamed "liberty sandwiches."

Once the United States entered the war on April 7, 1917, everyone was required to contribute, as government posters demanded. Those at home, eligible neither for military service nor munitions work in factories, could play their part by consuming less and buying war bonds.

World War I cost the federal government $30 billion. The bond system introduced to offset some of this expenditure was based on the successful strategy of European governments in wartime. War bonds, known as Liberty Bonds, were issued by the government to finance its wartime operations while avoiding high tax increases. During this war, American Liberty Bond posters raised approximately $17 billion. Posters were critical to this effort: a poster for the Second Liberty Loan of 1917 by Sackett & Wilhelms Corporation, for example, asked the public to "Remember Your First Thrill of American Liberty" and reminded them it is "Your Duty—Buy United States Government Bonds." And in 1918, a Liberty Bond poster by cartoonist Winsor McCay reminded Americans that "If You Can't Enlist—Invest! . . . Defend Your Country with Your Dollars!" Such designs played on the guilt and fear of Americans who were waiting at home while their fellow citizens fought in the trenches of France and Belgium. Often, like Pennell's poster, they also evoked the American way of life and the values that were at risk.

For the Fourth Liberty Loan Campaign, promoted in Pennell's poster *That Liberty Shall Not Perish from the Earth*, the movie star Douglas Fairbanks Sr. sold Liberty Bonds on Wall Street in New York. He not only matched an existing pledge for $1 million but also raised an additional $5 million. Even the Boy and Girl Scouts sold bonds in New York, enticing patrons with the slogan "Every Scout to Save a Soldier."

That Liberty Shall Not Perish from the Earth depicts New York Harbor engulfed in flames and relates to some of the imagery in the charcoal-and-ink drawings Pennell made at the front in France for the publication he ultimately abandoned. It was not hard for him to imagine the collapse of this iconic skyline on the basis of these experiences, and it is quite different from the majority of American wartime posters produced by his contemporaries.

Most notably, Pennell presents a scene of apocalyptic destruction rather than a tribute to American courage, democracy, and innovation. In this horrific image, the Statue of Liberty burns and crumbles against the harbor and city skyline, both aflame. The message is clear: if the enemy is not defeated, America and its values will be decisively extinguished.

It should also be noted here that while Pennell was a patriot, he was also a self-declared racist and an anti-Semite. While in college, he and a group of students mercilessly bullied Black artist and fellow student Henry Ossawa Tanner, tying him to an easel and subjecting him to a mock crucifixion. Pennell records the attack in his 1925 autobiography *The Adventures of An Illustrator* in a narrative that makes no secret of his racism. His anti-Semitism is no less evident in his distasteful 1892 publication *The Jew at Home: Impressions of a Summer and Autumn Spent with Him*. If his wartime poster clearly champions democratic American values, his writings indicate that in his own dealings with people, they did not amount to much.

LADY LIBERTY

The Statue of Liberty is 305 feet tall from the base of its pedestal to the top of its torch. At the time of its construction, it was the tallest structure not only in New York City, but also in the entire country. It held this status until the World Building was completed in 1890, surpassing the statue's height by just a few feet. The Statue of Liberty was built with an interior iron skeleton, technology that was being used at the same time on skyscrapers. Although it was not the first landmark in New York City's skyline, it was raised during a construction boom that lasted through the Great Depression. In spite of its renown, however, the Statue of Liberty was not declared a National Monument until 1924.

New York/The Wonder City of the World, 1927

Adolph Treidler (1886–1981)
The Collection of Berick Treidler & Lian Dolan
Image Courtesy of Poster House

- This poster shows a dramatic nighttime view of the tip of Manhattan behind the Statue of Liberty. Although several structures are identifiable in silhouette (including the Singer Building and the Woolworth Building), this is the first poster to present the cityscape at night as a single entity, one that would soon become iconic in such images.

- From Manhattan's early days as a Dutch settlement, ferries plied the waterways around it. This poster most likely shows the *Gowanus*, the *Nassau*, or the *Bay Ridge*—all single-funnel ferries commissioned in 1907, and each eventually scrapped in 1940.

- In 1927, this poster won Second Honorable Mention within the Posters and Car Cards category in the Art Directors Club's Sixth Annual of Advertising Art.

NEW YORK
The WONDER CITY of the WORLD
NEW YORK CENTRAL LINES

NEW YORK
invites you!

Go
PENNSYLVANIA RAILROAD

LEFT

New York/Pennsylvania Railroad, 1934

Designer Unknown
Image Courtesy of Swann Auction Galleries

- In contrast to the posters for shipping companies, which tended to present their most celebrated vessels, there is no sign of a train in this advertisement for the Pennsylvania Railroad. Instead, it entices viewers to travel with a dramatic image of New York that combines the city's most iconic symbols.

- From 1910, only the Pennsylvania Railroad Company and New York Central Line allowed travelers to reach Manhattan Island without getting off the train and taking a ferry. When this poster was published, passengers would have arrived at the elegant neo-classical building that then housed Pennsylvania Station (it was demolished between 1963 and 1966) after traveling in one of the many cars that made up what the railroad boasted was the "largest fleet of air-conditioned trains in the world."

- During this period, competition from cars and the economic collapse of the Great Depression had forced many railroads to merge, but the Pennsylvania Railroad, which owned all or part of some eight hundred other railroads, actually reinforced its position. Between 1931 and 1940, it expanded its electrified rail lines, partly with loans from the government's Reconstruction Finance Corporation, improving speeds between major cities. In 1935, its Broadway Limited, a premium-fare, all-sleeper service with an open-platform observation deck, had cut the journey time between Chicago and New York to sixteen and a half hours.

OPPOSITE

North America Express/ Italian Line, 1935

Renato Cenni (1906–77)
Image Courtesy of Alessandro Bellenda / Galleria L'Image, Alassio - Italy

- In this bold composition, the Statue of Liberty, silhouetted against the water with her back to the viewer, appears to be waving farewell to the ocean liner the SS *Rex* as it departs New York Harbor. This is the English-language variant of the poster; it was also issued in German.

- Italian Line (officially Italia di Navigazione SpA) began regular transatlantic operations between Italy and the United States in 1932. It was based on a merger of three Italian shipping companies, one of which was Trieste-based Cosulich STN mentioned on the poster. By that time, the company had already commissioned two new very luxurious, high-speed ocean liners, promoted as "the Rivieras afloat"—the SS *Rex* and the SS *Conte di Savoia*— both of which made frequent trips to New York. These two were among the many Italian Line vessels lost during World War II.

- The tourist class of the *Rex* was especially designed with middle-class American travelers in mind, and the ship made numerous transatlantic trips until 1940, which significantly boosted the Italian tourist trade. The liner was also a subject of national pride for the Italian dictator Benito Mussolini. In 1933, the *Rex* snatched the Blue Riband (an unofficial award for the passenger liner crossing the Atlantic with the highest average speed) from the German liner the SS *Bremen*.

- But during the 1930s, it also carried some thirty thousand Jewish passengers fleeing Fascism in Europe. The *Rex* was one of the Italian Line ships that, in spite of anti-Semitic legislation in Italy during this period, welcomed Jewish passengers to its neutral ships and installed a kosher kitchen. These had been installed on the liners of various shipping companies from about 1904, including White Star's *Titanic*.

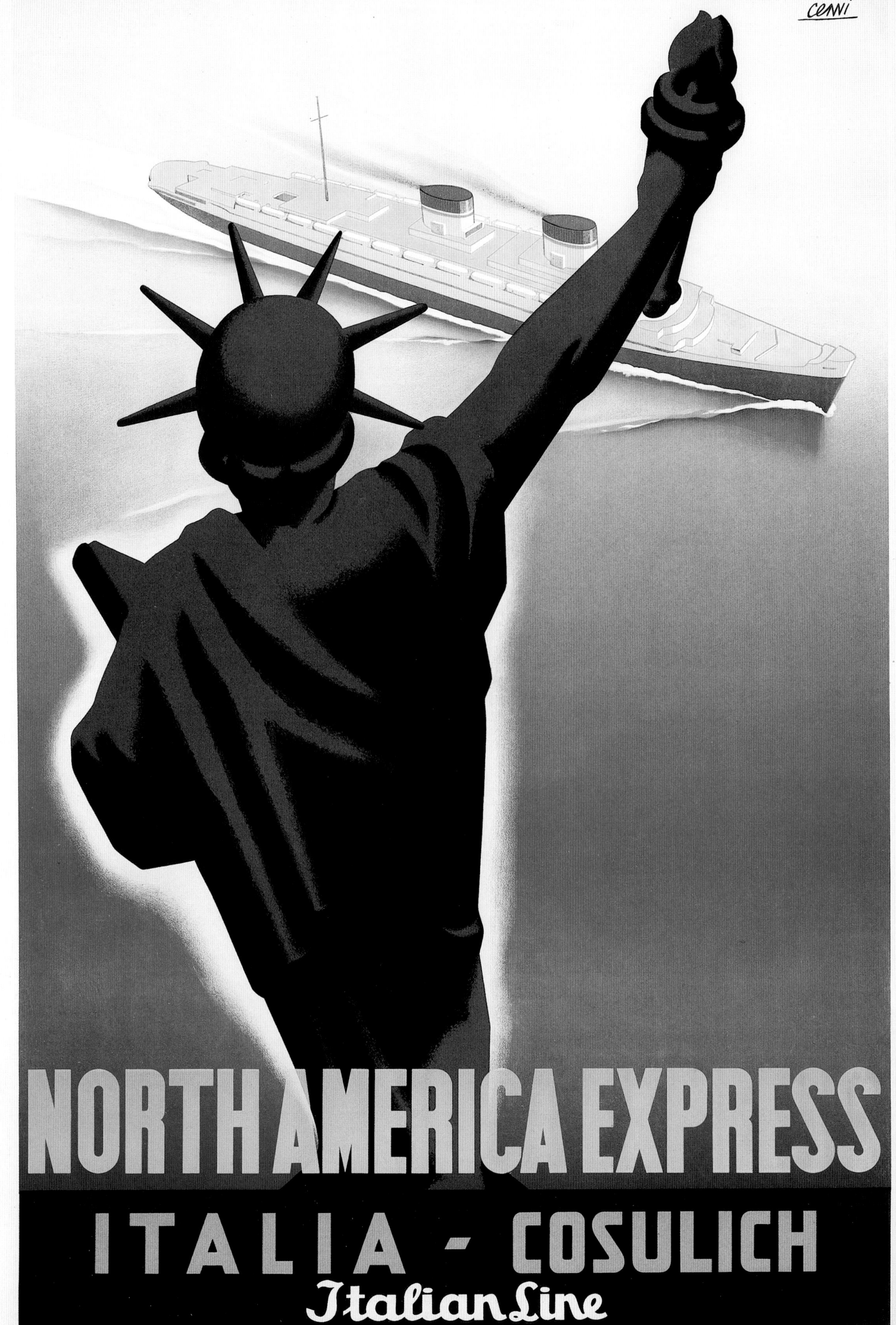
CENNI
NORTH AMERICA EXPRESS
ITALIA - COSULICH
Italian Line

New York Central System/ We Shall Not Fail, 1943

Leslie Ragan (1897–1972)
Image Courtesy of Swann Auction Galleries

- In this poster by Leslie Ragan, published during World War II, the Statue of Liberty promotes the patriotic contributions of the New York Central System railroad. She rides on top of one of its trains, her lit torch a beacon of hope held aloft against the night sky, as the train's head-lamp lights the way to victory.

- Railroads like the New York Central System, which connected New York and Boston to Montreal, Chicago, and St. Louis, played a critical role in the war effort. The number of rail passengers peaked during World War II, as did the record for rail freight. During this time, the railroads carried both domestic and military cargo, as well as transported soldiers and sailors around the country. As men were drafted, women and retirees were brought in to keep the trains running.

- The statement "We Shall Not Fail" is quoted from Winston Churchill's wartime radio broadcast on February 9, 1941: "We shall not fail or falter. We shall not weaken or tire. . . . Give us the tools, and we will finish the job." His words, in turn, echoed those of Abraham Lincoln in his 1858 House Divided speech at the Republican State Convention in Illinois: "We shall not fail—if we stand firm, we shall not fail."

Italia/Mediterranean–New York, c. 1948

Dario Bernazzoli (1908–99)
Image Courtesy of Swann Auction Galleries

- The enlarged, shadowy figure of the Statue of Liberty looms above the stylized Manhattan skyline, apparently waving goodbye to an Italian Line ship as it begins its journey across the Atlantic. The company had lost many of its ocean liners during the war but resumed commercial service in 1947. Around that time, the four of its vessels captured by the United States were also returned to it.

- This was one of many modernist designs produced by Bernazzoli for Italian Line and the other shipping companies that were among his main clients. He had apprenticed with the distinguished Genovese lithography firm of Barabino e Graeve, well-known for its travel posters, and opened his own graphic design studio in Genoa during the late 1930s.

OPPOSITE

New York/United Air Lines,
c. 1948

William Lawson (Dates Unknown)
Image Courtesy of Affiche Passion

- The Statue of Liberty stands here alone, without the usual cityscape behind her. Lawson represents the three disparate parts of the complex on Liberty Island: the statue itself, the elegant Beaux Arts base designed by Richard Morris Hunt between 1881 and 1886, and the former Fort Wood, which had the shape of an eleven-point star below it. The composition is bisected diagonally by the silver wing of a United Air Lines (restyled as United Airlines in 1975) plane, with its distinctive red, white, and blue markings.

- In the early 1930s, United had pioneered the Main Line route from New York to San Francisco via Chicago. In 1937, the airline had purchased its first Douglas DC-3s and painted "The Mainliner" on each of their fuselages as part of a new marketing plan. From then on, these Mainliners carried increasing numbers of domestic passengers as air travel began to rival railroads and cars. In 1947, United introduced the Douglas DC-6 Mainliner, presumably the plane glimpsed here. The DC-6 had originally been designed by the Douglas Aircraft Company for military purposes during the war but was adapted to long-range commercial travel soon after it ended.

- Little is known about the artist, William Lawson, but he appears to have designed posters for United for some twenty years, promoting its coast-to-coast service as well as other domestic destinations.

ABOVE

Fly BCPA to America, c. 1950

Designer Unknown
Image Courtesy of Affiche Passion

- This evocative design shows the Statue of Liberty guarding the entrance to New York Harbor and the glittering city beyond as a British Commonwealth Pacific Airlines (BCPA) plane, a Douglas DC-6, flies across the evening sky.

- BCPA was a short-lived company headquartered in Sydney and formed by the governments of Australia, New Zealand, and Great Britain in 1946 to allow trans-Pacific flights. While the adoption at the end of 1948 of the DC-6, an aircraft known for its incomparable reliability and operational efficiency, had given BCPA a brief (and unlikely) advantage over Pan Am on Pacific routes, it ultimately struggled against the various requirements of its three government owners. In 1954, BCPA was taken over by Qantas Empire Airways.

New York/Swissair, 1951

Henri Ott (1919–2009)
Private Collection, New York
Image Courtesy of Poster House

- This is part of a series of linocut posters designed by Henri Ott for Swissair in the 1950s.

- Ott's colorful interpretation of New York City at night is one of the earliest mid-century modernist views of the city's skyline in a poster. He was clearly not attempting to create a realistic image of the skyline as none of the buildings are identifiable; instead, the city's structures and lights are represented as an abstract entity.

- The neon Pepsi-Cola sign is the only recognizable landmark behind the Statue of Liberty—an unexpected and likely unsolicited product placement. As it was installed in Long Island City on top of a bottling plant in 1940, the sign would not have been visible from the Statue of Liberty, nor was it on top of a tall building as depicted here. As of 2003, it is permanently situated in Long Island City's Gantry Plaza State Park and can be seen from East Side, Manhattan. In 2016, it was granted official landmark status.

New York/Pan American, 1955

Alberta Amspoker (1926–2002)
Image Courtesy of The Ross Art Group Inc.

- This is one of a popular series of about twenty posters designed for Pan Am by (the otherwise little-known) Alberta Amspoker between 1955 and 1958. Unusually for airline posters of the period, these compositions did not typically show all or even part of an actual plane.

- Like most of Amspoker's poster designs, it is dominated by a single symbol of the particular location set against a plain ground, in this case, the head and neck of (a slightly grim-looking) Statue of Liberty in shades of gray. The cheerful, colorfully dressed tourists waving from her crown draw the eye up to a level just above the words "NEW YORK."

- Pan American Airways (commonly known as Pan Am), founded in 1927, was headquartered in Manhattan.

Between 1931 and 1942, it was the only international carrier in the United States, making New York a center of international aviation. Scheduled transatlantic passenger service began on a Pan Am flight from New York in June 1939, provided by a Boeing 314 seaplane called the *Dixie Clipper*; its service around the world was introduced in 1947 and it inaugurated the first commercial jet services from New York to Paris and London in 1958. Pan Am remained the major US airline until the early 1980s.

New York/Northwest Airlines, c. 1955

Dean P. Wessel (1920–2004)
Library of Congress, Prints & Photographs Division,
[LC-DIG-ds-11696]

- The iconic New York symbols that featured in so many travel posters only just hold their own against the large, colorful letters of the typography. In this poster, a pale, monochromatic Statue of Liberty stands on the right, while behind her, the New York City skyline is reduced to a geometric outline.

- The plane flying above the statue is the Boeing 377 Stratocruiser, a propeller-driven aircraft that was larger and more luxurious than the Douglas DC-6 and the Lockheed Constellation. With two decks, the 377 was very comfortable—but notoriously uneconomical and unreliable. Northwest Airlines's Stratocruisers began serving New York in late 1950, but they were phased out by September 1960 in favor of Douglas DC-8 jets and other more modern planes.

- Northwest Airlines was founded in 1926 as a mail service from Minneapolis/St. Paul to Chicago; it introduced passenger service the following year, which ultimately expanded throughout the region. Northwest's first New York service was launched in 1945. The airline merged with Delta in 2008, and then operated under the Delta name.

NEW YORK

ALLEGHENY AIRLINES

New York/Allegheny Airlines,
c. 1955

Designer Unknown
*Library of Congress, Prints
& Photographs Division,*
[LC-USZC4-13616]

• As in many of the posters, the Statue
of Liberty and a stylized Manhattan
skyline together represent the great
city of New York. Notably, however,

this one also features the new United
Nations Secretariat Building on the East
River, completed in 1951. The New York
location of the UN emphasized the key
role the United States was to play in
the organization. Here, the neutral form
of this International Style building with
its many national flags also serves as
a welcoming beacon to visitors arriving
from numerous countries.

• Allegheny was one of many forerunners
of the airline that finally took the name
US Airways in 1997. The airline operated
out of Pittsburgh, Pennsylvania, between
1952 and 1979, primarily on East Coast
routes. US Airways completed its last
flight in 2015, soon after its merger with
American Airlines.

FLY TWA
TRANS WORLD AIRLINES

TWA/New York, c. 1957

David Klein (1918–2005)
Image Courtesy of Swann Auction Galleries

- The rather stark image in this poster, showing the upper part of the Statue of Liberty against the blue sky, features one of the old propeller-driven planes, powered by piston engines, that were phased out by TWA in 1959 in favor of jet planes.

- David Klein worked as a designer for TWA (Trans World Airlines) from the late 1950s through the 1960s. By this time, the airline was favored by celebrities and movie stars, and even less-elevated beings were increasingly likely to cross the Atlantic by air than by ship. The fact that between 1939 and 1966 it was owned by Howard Hughes, the celebrated billionaire aviator, film producer, and businessman, probably contributed much to the airline's perceived glamour.

OPPOSITE

New York/Delta Air Lines, 1957

William G. Slattery (1929–97)
Image Courtesy of Swann Auction Galleries

- During the 1950s, Delta Air Lines, founded as an aerial crop-dusting company called Huff Daland Dusters in 1925, expanded its domestic routes from its hub in Atlanta and began offering international passage to the Caribbean and Caracas.

- Clearly, the airline's promotional needs had radically expanded. South African–born artist and graphic designer William Slattery was hired by the Atlanta advertising agency Burke Dowling Adams to create a series of posters for Delta, its most important client. This was completed in 1957 and the posters were displayed around the United States until 1961.

- In this composition from the series, Slattery incorporates the two classic New York symbols of the Statue of Liberty and the skyline (with the Empire State Building in red at the center) in a typically colorful and humorous design. The caricatured head of the statue even appears to be smiling slightly.

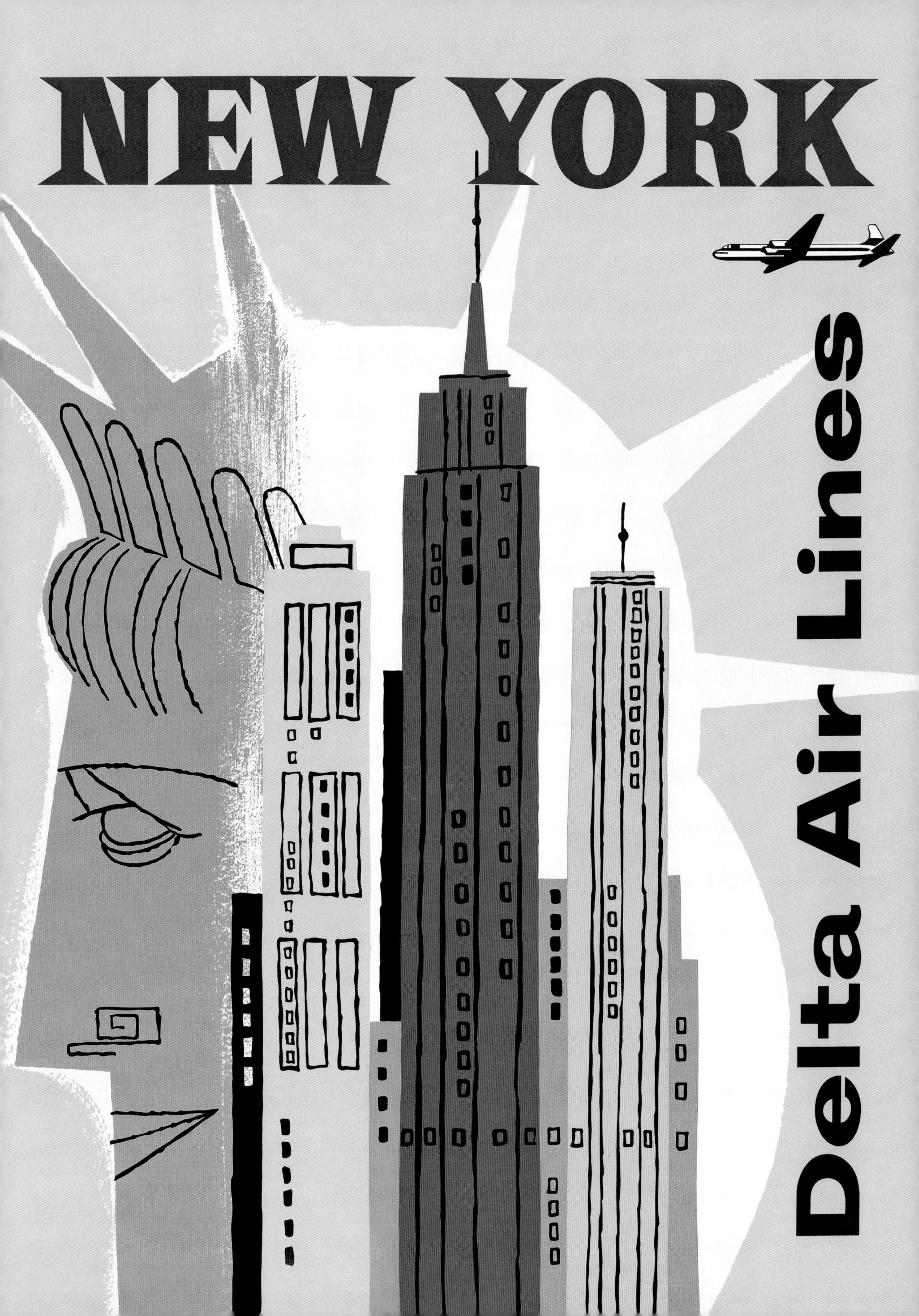
NEW YORK
Delta Air Lines

New York/United Air Lines, c. 1960

Stanley Walter Galli (1912–2009)
Private Collection, New York
Image Courtesy of Poster House

- This poster shows the top of the Statue of Liberty facing southeast to welcome ships approaching New York Harbor from the Atlantic.

- As the statue has her back to the city, visitors to the crown, with its twenty-five windows and seven spikes, cannot actually see the skyscrapers of Lower Manhattan.

- In addition to using the skyscrapers as a point of perspective, Stanley Galli also set three seagulls against the statue to emphasize its enormous size, an effect that appears to reference an element in A. M. Cassandre's celebrated poster design of 1935, in which he shows a flock of seagulls against the hull of the giant ocean liner the SS *Normandie*.

- After the terror attacks of September 11, 2001, the crown was closed to the public and only reopened in October 2022.

Paris–New York/Lignes Aeriennes Irlandaises, c. 1959

Designer Unknown
Collection Galerie 1 2 3 -
Geneva/Switzerland
www.galerie123.com

- In addition to the familiar motif of the Statue of Liberty in front of the city skyline, this poster shows the airline's Lockheed Super Constellation. The fourteen-hour journey from Ireland to New York would have been long but very comfortable since the "Connie," as it was known, was large, powerful, and fully pressurized.

- In April 1958, the inaugural flight from Shannon, Ireland, to New York was greeted on the tarmac by a salute from the 165th Infantry of the New York National Guard. The airline carried some fifteen thousand passengers to and fro between Ireland and New York in its first year of transatlantic operation. While some of these would certainly have been tourists, the majority were emigrants from Ireland who wished to join family members already resident in the United States.

New York/Eastern Air Lines,
c. 1960

Designer Unknown
*Poster Photo Archives, Posters Please,
Inc., NYC*

- This poster is based on a photograph
  in which the Statue of Liberty is seen,
  unusually for such designs, from below.
  It allows a good view of Richard Morris
  Hunt's Beaux Arts base for the statue.

- Between the 1930s and the '50s, most
  major airlines focused on domestic
  routes. Eastern Air Lines sought to
  dominate air travel between north-
  eastern cities, especially New York,
  and the vacation destinations of
  Florida and the South under the
  tagline "Number one to the sun."
  Economic troubles forced its closure
  in 1991.

- The company, founded in Pennsylvania
  in 1926 as an airmail service called
  Pitcairn Aviation, was renamed Eastern
  Air Transport in 1930. After the Air Mail
  Act of 1934 forced a restructuring of the
  airlines to break up monopolies, it was
  finally named Eastern Air Lines.

Fly TWA Jets, c. 1960

David Klein (1918–2005)
Private Collection, New York
Image Courtesy of Poster House

- This poster presents the Statue of Liberty swathed in a swirl of multicolored starbursts. They might be intended to represent fireworks, the reflection of the city's lights in the water, or the contrails of a jet flying overhead.

Regardless, the design is an exuberant celebration of Lady Liberty.

- The sculptor Frédéric Auguste Bartholdi had originally wanted the torch to be formed from sheets of gilded copper so that it could be illuminated by external lights, but before its inauguration in 1886, nine arc lamps were inserted within the torch as requested by the US Lighthouse Board. The lamps were permanently extinguished in 1902.

- From the late 1950s through the '60s, David Klein designed dozens of posters for TWA spanning an array of styles, from mid-century modernism to narrative illustration to, as shown here, abstract proto-psychedelia.

ALITALIA AIRLINES

NEW YORK

Alitalia Airlines/New York,
c. 1960

Designer Unknown
*Image Courtesy of Alessandro Bellenda /
Galleria L'Image, Alassio - Italy*

- This is one of a series of posters designed for Alitalia in the early 1960s, each showing a single shadowy motif symbolizing the specific destination. Tokyo is represented by a geisha, for example; London by a member of the King's Guard in a bearskin hat; and Rome by the Spanish Steps.

- By this time, Alitalia, founded in 1946 as Aerolinee Italiane Internazionali, was in its heyday. Passengers to New York would have flown in comfort on one of its DC-8 jets, which it advertised as "the most powerful airliner aloft!" The planes now offered a new level of luxury and elegance: they were restyled with leather and wood fittings, and stewardesses in uniforms designed by the celebrated Roman fashion house of Sorelle Fontana offered Italian food and wine.

American Airlines/New York, 1964

Webber (Dates Unknown)
Image Courtesy of Swann Auction Galleries

- The stylized form of the Statue of Liberty and the colorful patchwork jumble of the cityscape dominate the image here. The plane and the ocean liner in the background emphasize the bustling city's role as a magnet for both tourism and trade.

- The poster was made during a heyday for American Airlines. The company had successfully begun to offer transcontinental jet service on Boeing 707s in 1959, enabling speedier and safer flights. In 1960, it had made its largest base in New York, building a major terminal at Idlewild Airport (now John F. Kennedy Airport). And in 1960, it had installed Sabre, the first fully electronic booking service, significantly increasing its share of the market and revolutionizing the industry. It also made history the same year when it hired Dave Harris, the first African American pilot to fly for a major commercial airline.

New York/Fly TWA, c. 1965

David Klein (1918–2005)
Poster Photo Archives, Posters Please, Inc., NYC

- Here, the Statue of Liberty, restyled with the face and bangs of a modern woman, dominates an image incorporating such New York City landmarks as St. Patrick's Cathedral and the Brooklyn Bridge, the statue of Christopher Columbus at Columbus Circle (on the far right), and the statue of George Washington found at Federal Hall (on the far left).

- The tiny plane seen at upper left, a typical feature of Klein's designs for TWA, is one of the new Boeing 707 jet planes put into service by the airline

in March 1959. American Airlines had already introduced coast-to-coast jet passenger service in January of that year, and TWA scrambled to offer the same service. The Boeing 707 could fly at greater speeds and climb higher and faster than the old propeller-driven planes and soon revolutionized the industry, becoming standard on domestic and transatlantic flights during the 1960s.

- Klein, who also illustrated posters for such travel companies as Cunard, Amtrak, and Holland America Line, earned numerous awards for his designs. He played a critical role in the effective branding of TWA during this period, creating striking posters that typically present a city's iconic landmarks in bright colors combined with minimal text.

AMERICAN AIRLINES
NEW YORK

New York

△ DELTA AIR LINES

- The reliably sturdy form of the Statue of Liberty in this psychedelic poster contrasts with the relaxed pose of the young woman apparently reveling in all the city has to offer as she emerges from behind the tumbling skyscrapers. The image is clearly intended to appeal to youthful, impecunious travelers from all over America with dreams of traveling to New York.

- Curiously, however, a large steamship, rather than a Greyhound bus, dominates the foreground of the composition. Perhaps the racing greyhound logo at lower right is intended to suggest the fact that traveling by bus, rather than by lumbering ocean liner, will get to New York much more quickly.

- Jack Laycox was a California artist who also worked as a commercial illustrator. During the 1970s, he was commissioned by Delta Air Lines to design a series of posters. The painterly quality of these impressionistic compositions, with their blobs and drips of color defining and highlighting many of the details, is informed by the style of the works in oil and watercolor he continued to produce throughout his career.

- The image shows a view up the East River, as indicated by the sketchy form of the Brooklyn Bridge in the distance.

NEW YORK BY RAIL

During the 1920s and '30s—the golden age of domestic rail travel in the United States— train companies in the Northeast created advertisements that predominantly focused on individual sights: points of progress, pride, and accomplishment within the city, as well as architectural highlights and evidence of modern innovation along their routes. European travel posters of the same era typically emphasized centuries-old cathedrals or beautiful natural vistas, but for the American domestic market, railroads promoted symbols of prowess, power, and pride. Although such posters were primarily designed to sell train tickets by encouraging travelers to visit the metropolis, they simultaneously glorified the ambitious urban projects financed by the railroad magnates and titans of American industry whose ambitions had helped to shape the city.

GRAND CENTRAL TERMINAL
NEW YORK
The Gateway to a Continent

NEW YORK CENTRAL LINES

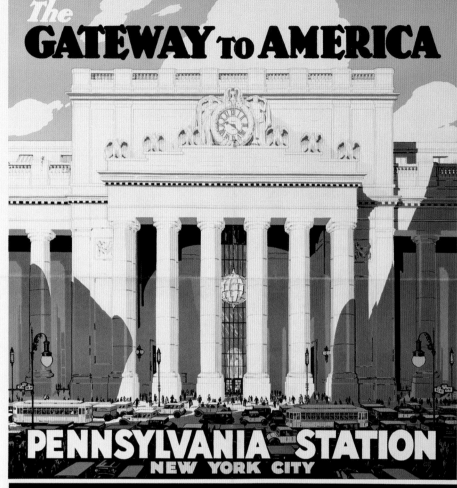

PENNSYLVANIA
RAILROAD

The
GATEWAY to AMERICA

PENNSYLVANIA STATION
NEW YORK CITY

From this splendid portal extend the main lines
of America's greatest railroad-with its own
and connecting services radiating to all
parts of the United States, Canada & Mexico.

WAGONS-LITS-COOK
WORLD TRAVEL ORGANIZATION
General Foreign Passenger Agents

**Pennsylvania Railroad/
The Gateway to America**, 1929

Ivar Gull (Dates Unknown)
*Poster House Permanent Collection
Image Courtesy of Poster House*

- Ground was broken for Pennsylvania Station in 1904, and construction began two years later; the McKim, Mead & White masterpiece finally opened in 1910. This is one of the only posters depicting the architectural icon.

- Once the Pennsylvania Railroad began to invest in electrification to lower operating costs and meet the requirements of smoke-abatement laws in cities that it served, construction on underwater tunnels became possible, allowing it to link New Jersey with Midtown Manhattan. The building covered two city blocks between Seventh and Eighth Avenues and Thirty-First and Thirty-Third Streets.

- The term "Gateway to America" was originally used to describe Ellis Island and was chosen by the Pennsylvania Railroad as a counterpoint to New York Central Railroad's slogan asserting that Grand Central Terminal was the "Gateway to a Continent."

- From the 1920s, the Pennsylvania Railroad began commissioning exceptional posters, a number of which were designed by Ivar Gull, who also illustrated its timetables. This poster was left blank in the lower register so travel agencies could overprint their own information.

New York Central Building, 1930

Chesley Bonestell (1888–1986)
*Collection of Jolean & David Breger
Image Courtesy of Poster House*

- Before Grand Central Terminal was completed in 1913, the area between Forty-Fifth and Forty-Eighth Streets was an exposed trainyard. To create the terminal, extensive excavation allowed the tracks, platforms, and train shed to be constructed underground, while the area aboveground could be developed, a commercial urban project referred to as Terminal City. Numerous hotels (including the Biltmore, the Commodore, and the still-extant Roosevelt), a post office, and apartment and office buildings were included in this ambitious new plan.

- The New York Central Building (known today as the Helmsley Building) straddles Park Avenue and was built on the area above the Grand Central train yard. Constructed between 1927 and 1929, it was the corporate seat of the railroad company and the last significant addition to Terminal City.

NEW YORK CENTRAL BUILDING

PARK AVENUE, NEW YORK

AT · THE · GATEWAY · TO · A · CONTINENT

FIFTH AVENUE · NEW YORK
The World's Greatest Shopping Street
TRAVEL BY TRAIN

Fifth Avenue/New York, 1932

Frederic Kimball Mizen (1888–1964)
Collection of Jolean & David Breger
Image Courtesy of Poster House

- The Empire State Building opened in May 1931, and was constructed in just over thirteen months. The antenna so associated with its silhouette today was not added until 1951, bringing its height to 1,472 feet.

- This poster was printed shortly after the skyscraper's completion and is most likely its earliest appearance on a poster.

- During the 1930s, a group of thirty railroads created the "Travel by Train" campaign, hoping to counter the growing popularity of the automobile. The coalition produced around a dozen posters highlighting major destinations around the country, none of which promote a specific train company.

- With the exception of Marble Collegiate Church's spire on Twenty-Ninth Street, this view of Fifth Avenue is not architecturally accurate. It does, however, showcase the Fifth Avenue Coach Company's double-decker buses and the fact that the street had two-way traffic—which it did until 1966.

New York/Reading Railway System, c. 1932

Designer Unknown
© *David Pollack Vintage Posters*

- This seldom-seen poster for the Reading Railway System highlights One Wall Street, the Art Deco masterpiece, as it glistens in golden-hour sunshine. In reality, such a glow was unlikely as the building's facade is made of limestone.

- Also visible here are the Manhattan Company Building surmounted by a pyramid-shaped roof at the left, and the much shorter Bankers Trust Building with a similar roof directly below it.

- The Reading Railway System was one of the names used by the Reading

Company, a Philadelphia-based organization that operated from 1924 until it became part of Conrail in 1976. Its predecessor was founded in 1833, allowing the poster's claim that Reading had offered "Nearly a Century of Service."

- In order to compete with the Pennsylvania Railroad and the Baltimore & Ohio Railroad, the Philadelphia & Reading Railroad drew attention to its "every hour on the hour" service—a higher frequency between Philadelphia and New York City than was offered by its rivals. As the Reading Railway controlled the Jersey Central Railroad, whose actual terminus was in Jersey City, however, passengers had to take a ferry into Manhattan once they reached that destination.

NEW YORK THE UPPER BAY FROM LOWER MANHATTAN

NEW YORK CENTRAL SYSTEM

New York/The Upper Bay from Lower Manhattan, 1935

Leslie Ragan (1897–1972)
Private Collection, New York
Image Courtesy of Poster House

- This poster shows a dramatic bird's-eye view of Battery Park, with New York Harbor, the Statue of Liberty, Ellis Island, and New Jersey in the background. Also visible are the roofs of the rectangular US Custom House and the New York Produce Exchange, as well as a sliver of the 741-foot-tall City Bank–Farmers Trust Building (known today as 20 Exchange Place) on the left and the ziggurat-style pyramid roof of the Standard Oil Building.

- The view is based on a photograph taken on April 13, 1933, by Percy Loomis Sperr from the observation deck of the Cities Service Building at 70 Pine Street in Manhattan's Financial District. The building—originally known as 60 Wall Tower—was constructed between 1930 and 1932.

- Sperr was a prolific photographer who documented New York as it underwent a period of great growth and change. Between the 1920s and the 1940s, he took more than thirty thousand photographs of the city.

Rockefeller Center/New York, c. 1935

Leslie Ragan (1897–1972)
Poster House Permanent Collection
Image Courtesy of Poster House

- This poster predates the completion of Rockefeller Center, which was built between 1931 and 1939. By 1936, the buildings depicted in the poster had already been constructed, yet Ragan's view is not an entirely accurate rendering of the complex since it includes several buildings that were not ultimately realized.

- Ragan frequently relied on preexisting artwork when designing posters. Here, he was most likely inspired by a promotional postcard that was issued before the project was completed and featured similarly constructed towers flanking the central RCA Building (known today as 30 Rockefeller Plaza). In the center's finished state, those structures are quite different; one is even oriented in the opposite direction. Also visible in the poster are seven roof gardens—only five were actually completed.

- The enormity of Rockefeller Center, shown here from a bird's-eye view, is emphasized by its comparison to St. Patrick's Cathedral in the foreground and the Hudson River and New Jersey in the distance, as well as by the impressive shadow it casts over neighboring buildings.

- The Gothic spire of St. Nicholas Collegiate Reformed Protestant Dutch Church is depicted at the corner of Forty-Eighth Street and Fifth Avenue at the lower left of the composition. It was razed in the summer of 1949 to make way for the Sinclair Building.

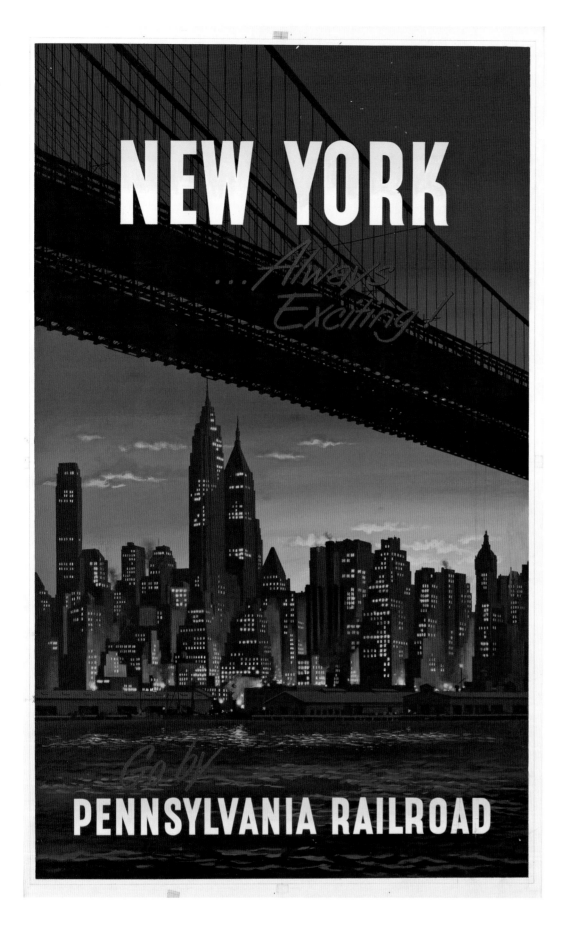

New York/Pennsylvania Railroad, c. 1940

Designer Unknown
Image Courtesy of Swann Auction Galleries

- This atmospheric evening view of the Lower East Side and Wall Street is only visible from the middle of the East River, from underneath the Brooklyn Bridge.

- The towers of the Cities Service Building at 70 Pine Street and the Manhattan Company Building at 40 Wall Street loom large in the distance, with the slightly shorter Bankers Trust Building at 14 Wall Street. To the far right is the Singer Building—once the world's tallest building, now over-shadowed by more ambitious new construction. At the far left is the City Bank–Farmers Trust Building.

- At the river level, the Fulton Fish Market and its associated docks are shown in shadow. The market opened in 1822, and stayed on the same site until 2005, when it moved to the Bronx. By the 1950s, most of the fish was brought in by truck rather than unloaded from the docks along the East River.

New York/Pennsylvania Railroad, c. 1950

Designer Unknown
Image Courtesy of Swann Auction Galleries

- Like the other posters for the Pennsylvania Railroad, this image showcases the towers of the Financial District, but from a slightly different angle. Shown from the left are the Standard Oil Building at 26 Broadway, the City Bank–Farmers Trust Building at 20 Exchange Place, the Cities Service Building at 70 Pine Street, the Manhattan Company Building at 40 Wall Street, the Irving Trust Company Building at 1 Wall Street, and the Bankers Trust Building at 14 Wall Street.

- The foreground is dominated by one of the Pennsylvania Railroad's car-float operations in New York that moved freight to and from its yards in New Jersey to Manhattan by water.

New York/Pennsylvania Railroad, 1949

Designer Unknown
Image Courtesy of Swann Auction Galleries

- This pair of posters captures nearly identical views of Manhattan as seen from Governors Island at dawn and dusk. The exact same location was used as inspiration for both photographic images, as evidenced by the identical tree branches in the upper register of each composition.

- The contrast between the daytime logo and the bright, neon nighttime sign emphasizes Manhattan's reputation as a "work hard, play hard" city.

**New York/Pennsylvania
Railroad**, c. 1950

Designer Unknown
*Image Courtesy of Swann
Auction Galleries*

New York/Pennsylvania Railroad, 1952

Harley Wood (Dates Unknown)
Collection of Edward J. McCann

- In this poster for the Pennsylvania Railroad's service to New York City, a glamorous couple is shown enjoying the view toward downtown Manhattan from the top of the Empire State Building. The lighted avenues below seem to mimic rail lines like those in many classic French railway posters, turning the terrace of the building into a romantic caboose at the back of a train.

- Interestingly, the poster fails to include the safety fence that was installed around the building's perimeter in 1947 after a series of attempted suicides.

- The Pennsylvania Railroad was not alone in using the "Go by Train" tagline on its posters; various American, British, and Australian train companies also used it to broadly encourage rail travel.

- This view proved popular for the company; it used it in more photographic detail for the poster seen to the right, which was produced about a decade later (but without the couple), as well as for the covers of its timetables.

New York/Pennsylvania Railroad, c. 1964

Designer Unknown
Image Courtesy of Swann Auction Galleries

- This daytime view from the top of the Empire State Building mimics the composition of the earlier, more romantic version by Harley Wood. Unlike that design, however, this one was based on an enlarged, colorized photograph rather than on an illustration, a more technologically advanced technique.

- Like the earlier design, this poster highlights three main arterial avenues within Manhattan: Fifth Avenue, Broadway, and Sixth Avenue, all leading downtown.

- At the time, promotional material for the Empire State Building boasted that on a clear day, visitors could see as far as eighty miles away, allowing a view not only of New York State but also glimpses of New Jersey, Connecticut, Pennsylvania, and Massachusetts. Here, the photograph shows the many famous towers of the Wall Street district as well as the Flatiron Building at 175 Fifth Avenue (originally the Fuller Building) at the lower center of the image, and the Metropolitan Life Building (once the world's tallest building) and its annex at the lower left.

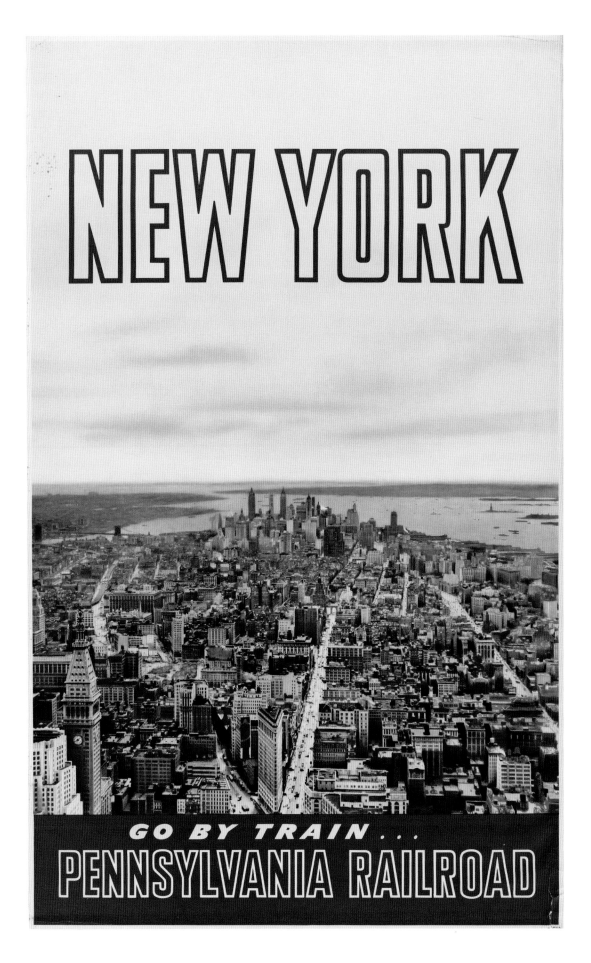

NEW YORK

GO BY TRAIN . . .
PENNSYLVANIA RAILROAD

SOFT LIGHT, BIG CITY: LESLIE RAGAN'S NEW YORK POSTERS

BY COLETTE GAITER

> "Ultimately, to satisfy the desires of tourists and tourism promoters, New York had to be seen and marketed as *both* American and un-American, treading a fine line between the bold display of difference and the reassuring show of sameness."
> —Art M. Blake

eslie Ragan's illustrations for the New York Central System train line helped change the popular image of New York City throughout the United States, successfully promoting the metropolis as a desirable travel destination. His efforts continued a deliberate campaign to enhance the city's widespread appeal and reflected an organic shift in the perception of the city that had begun during the last decades of the nineteenth century and had only been accelerated by World War II. By the 1950s, New York was considered less an outlier compared to other cities, and more an American treasure. It had gradually emerged as an essentially American city offering experiences from around the world. The popular fear of density and crime was superseded to some extent by the sense that New York was an epicenter of commerce and international culture, one accessible without the need to cross a border or an ocean.

Ragan, born in Iowa, began his career during the 1920s creating illustrations for the South Shore Line that traveled through the American heartland below Lake Michigan, between cities like Chicago and Cleveland. These drawings provided the stylistic basis for the poster designs he made in New York in the 1930s and '40s.

In his compositions, Ragan used familiar pastel and muted earth tones to describe the sky and the buildings, softening the hard-edged outlines of the city's streetscapes seen in the black-and-white photographs of these decades. It could be argued that such photographs did New York the greatest disservice by imprinting cold, colorless, and lifeless images onto people's minds. Ragan's quasi-realistic and romantic illustrations made the city more appealing to visitors who might never have seen a skyscraper. During the 1930s, when Ragan created most of his posters, black-and-white photographs of New York—by William Frange and Berenice Abbott, for example—showed gray rectangles of various heights clustered in dense city blocks that look like children's building toys. From the sky, Midtown Manhattan looked smoggy and monotonous. Perhaps such images contributed to the frequent criticisms of New York that appeared in the national press. They also conjured the city in Fritz Lang's then-controversial 1927 film *Metropolis*, a soulless, futurist dystopia ruled by merciless industrialists and characterized by towering skyscrapers (see pages 78–79). By contrast, Ragan's cityscapes suggested an optimistic surrealism. They paid homage to the technical ingenuity and prosperity that made these buildings possible, structures that seemed to rise directly from the waters surrounding them.

Unlike many advertisements of the time, Ragan's images generally excluded people. Most of his designs for the New York Central Line combined bucolic romanticism with scenes of modern train travel, visually bridging the real and imagined cultural gap between city and countryside. His sleek, streamlined trains and skyscrapers referenced a natural color palette, reflecting the sky and the landscape on their surfaces. Ragan's work also corresponded with the expansion of commercial illustration and advertising in the first decades of the twentieth century, when successful graphic designers like J.C. Leyendecker began to produce illustrations for posters, advertisements, books, and magazines. Advertising expanded alongside popular magazines and became the primary source of funding for most publications. This development in magazine advertising paralleled the introduction of what would now be seen as target marketing, using the psychology-based "science of visual persuasion," a strategy that became increasingly sophisticated as it incorporated a range of aspirational images.

There are many possible reasons that Ragan inserted so few people into his posters promoting rail travel. He probably realized it would be hard, given the diverse nature of the city's population, to represent a "typical" New Yorker. According to Michael Zega in *Travel by Train: The American Railroad Poster, 1870–1950* (2002), New York Central's advertising approach lay in "depicting the natural landscape and cities along its route." Ragan applied this fairly consistently in his work—highlighting the landscape rather than people, even when only showing buildings. People traveled to New York by train for business and pleasure, to flee an intolerable situation, or to seek their fortunes. The posters encouraged travelers to picture themselves in these luminous scenes without feeling a need to compare themselves to idealized passengers. In this sense, Ragan's posters sold possibility rather than identification or aspiration.

By the time Ragan began working in New York in 1929, the third major wave of immigration to the United States from Europe, involving some twenty-eight million people, was nearly complete. The conditions in which most of these new arrivals lived in the city were crowded and unsanitary, and they had to hustle to find whatever work they could in order to survive. This situation surely contributed to New York's reputation as dirty and dangerous, one that also reflected ingrained racism and xenophobia. During the 1930s, however, New York was also undeniably a rich center of immigrant culture—literary, artistic, and musical. It was multiracial and multicultural. It is fair to say that there is no evidence of any of this in Ragan's cheerful images of the city.

In the 2006 book *How New York Became American, 1890–1924*, Art M. Blake sees the dramatic landscapes of the mountainous American West as analogous to the "burgeoning capitalist market" that financed New York City skyscrapers—another kind of essential American landscape. Ragan's New York work started around 1929, and in about 1936, he created a poster for New York Central Line advertising Rockefeller Center, a complex that was mostly completed by 1935 (see page 71). This was just a few years after the completion of the Chrysler Building (1930) with its celebrated Art Deco spire, and the Empire State Building (1931) that soon surpassed it as the tallest building in the world, its more subtle Art Deco details viewable at ground level and in its interior. Here, Ragan recreated in muted earth tones the bird's-eye view of the massive Rockefeller Center tower from an architectural drawing by John Weinrich, transforming it into a warm and inviting scene. The scale remained true, but the colors softened the image of a Midtown Manhattan dominated by cold concrete and metal.

One of the things that those who dislike New York object to most is the relative lack of open space (apart from Central Park), the very thing that makes the city function efficiently. Gridded blocks containing tall buildings pack millions of people onto the relatively tiny island of Manhattan as they work, live, and play. Buses and an aged but indispensable subway system (invisible from street level) help people navigate the fairly short distances within Manhattan and out into the less densely populated boroughs. In an effort to redress this perception, perhaps, in his poster titled *New York: The Upper Bay from Lower Manhattan* (see page 70), Ragan gives more than half the space to water with a sprinkling of boats, a large park area, and distant land adjacent to the harbor. The Statue of Liberty can just be seen on the left. He mitigates the stark forms of the buildings in the foreground with color and softened light and edges, as he would do with the buildings in the Rockefeller Center poster. This bird's-eye view combines the kind of open vistas familiar to train travelers with a sense of the densely built environment of Lower Manhattan.

Once Ragan moved to New York City, the technical production methods used to make his posters began to change as his graphic style evolved. In his posters for the Midwestern South Shore Line, created in the 1920s, he had used solid areas of color to create the total image—almost like cut paper. These suggest children's storybook illustrations, composed with distinct, stylized, and simplified shapes. With these distilled forms and judicious use of tone, Ragan expanded on the figurative and illustrational tradition of American artists like Howard Pyle, Maxfield Parrish, and N.C. Wyeth.

The leaves on the trees, for example, are represented by organic shapes of green outlined with a thick, darker green border. The borders not only created an Art Nouveau effect but also assisted in the lithographic printing process. Each color in the image required a separate lithography stone. The thick borders in darker colors could serve to cover any mistakes in registering the images correctly after several passes through the printing press. A shift in the paper might leave empty spots on the page, so the printers typically overlapped the colors in a technique called *trapping*. However, Ragan and the printers he worked with later on for the New York Central Line posters developed a subtler technique. They made the borders thinner and replaced flat colors in distinct shapes with various colors layered on top of each other—using brushstrokes to create textures like those in actual paintings. All of this was achieved without the accuracy of contemporary photographic color separation, where filters extract each of the four process colors from a source document. The uniform sans-serif lettering on these New York City posters adds another layer of modernist style.

Almost one hundred years since Leslie Ragan created his first New York City posters, the Manhattan skyline remains a wonder to behold. It was even more impressive to new arrivals who had never before seen a big city—which included many Americans before World War II.

During the 1930s, many artists and designers fled Fascism in Europe and settled in the United States, introducing avant-garde modernism into graphic design. Joseph Binder, an immigrant Austrian artist and graphic designer, was one of many contemporaries who believed that the predominant American style of realistic representation belonged in the past and that modern design should be based on geometry and color.

From the perspective of such European modernists, Ragan's illustrations were certainly not avant-garde. He effectively evoked a sense of wonder at vast, sweeping landscapes and the modern technological marvel of cross-country train travel in a largely conventional, figurative style. As an emerging financial capital in the 1920s, the United States had the resources to build trains and structures as awe-inspiring as the great mountains of the American West. Ragan's poster designs celebrated the natural and urban grandeur that distinguished the country physically and ideologically from Europe, with its much older, more established cities. At the same time, his posters promoted that the best way to fully experience the country's spectacular vistas was through the windows of a sleek and powerful modern train.

NEW YORK FROM THE SEA

Transatlantic travel continued throughout the Great Depression, with many of the most luxurious ships still making the crossing. The stately RMS *Queen Mary* had been commissioned six months before the stock market crash of 1929, and while immigration to America continued, albeit at a much slower rate, advertising during these years focused more on well-to-do passengers. Poster designers depicted New York as an overwhelming, unbelievable city. Rather than showing some of the experiences visitors might have there, their compositions typically emphasized the sheer spectacle of the gigantic city. Ships took pride of place in designs that highlighted their size through dramatic perspectives that compared them to New York's towering skyscrapers, effectively suggesting that passengers might find the means of transport as impressive and enthralling as the destination.

- This early, abstract image of New York combines an immediately recognizable skyline with the stars and stripes and red, white, and blue of the American flag.

- As part of its reparations after World War I, Germany was required to surrender many of its ships to the Allies, and its shipping industry was decimated. The Royal Mail Line filled the commercial gap by providing service across the Atlantic from Hamburg through Cherbourg and Southampton, dominating the route through the 1920s. This British company promoted itself as "The Comfort Route" on its international services, implying class, attentiveness, courtesy, and elegance.

- This geometric, creative vision of the city was the inspiration for a number of other posters and magazine covers. It also appeared on brochures for the shipping line.

THE ROYAL MAIL LINE
TO
NEW YORK
MAKE YOUR NEXT CROSSING BY
"THE COMFORT ROUTE"

THE ROYAL MAIL STEAM PACKET CO
ATLANTIC HOUSE, MOORGATE, E.C.2

Cunard Line/Europe–America, c. 1925

Kenneth Denton Shoesmith
(1890–1939)
Image Courtesy of Swann Auction Galleries

- Ocean liners were the largest vessels most people had ever seen. Poster designers frequently emphasized their sheer scale by juxtaposing them with the other masterpieces of gigantic engineering of that period—skyscrapers. Here, Kenneth Denton Shoesmith, an artist who frequently designed posters for ships, sets the RMS *Aquitania* between two beautifully detailed towers, each window revealing its own small world within New York City.

- The *Aquitania* made its maiden voyage in 1914, shortly before the outbreak of World War I. Impressively, it could hold a thousand more passengers than either of its sister ships, the *Lusitania* and *Mauretania*. During the war, the *Aquitania* served as a troop carrier and floating hospital, resulting in a six-year hiatus from passenger service.

- The meaning behind Shoesmith's use of pink in this poster is twofold. During the Art Deco period, the color was often associated with urban modernism, effectively linking Cunard's service with cutting-edge sophistication. A pink sky also typically indicates an evening scene and suggests that the *Aquitania* is departing New York Harbor at sunset. The drama of this golden hour is increased by the reflection of the sky in the river, making the ship appear to be floating in air.

- In addition to being a maritime oil painter and poster designer for Royal Mail, Canadian Pacific, and Cunard, Shoesmith created many of the murals on board the RMS *Queen Mary*, launched in 1936.

Sunset Route
by Rail and Sea to New York
San Francisco
via
Los Angeles
and
New Orleans

SUNSET LIMITED

SOUTHERN PACIFIC LINES

Southern Pacific Lines

Southern Pacific/ Sunset Route, 1928

Michel Kady (1901–77)
Poster Photo Archives, Posters Please, Inc., NYC

- The Sunset Route was a combined rail-and-sea voyage offered by the Southern Pacific Railroad. The first half of the journey from San Francisco to New Orleans was by train, while the second half took passengers by steamship to New York.

- While the dominant, framed image in this poster focuses on a train departing San Francisco, the background presents the SS *Creole* against the Manhattan skyline, with the since-demolished Singer Tower on the far right.

- The rail portion of Southern Pacific's Sunset Route is now known as Amtrak's Sunset Limited, making this one of the most enduring railroad names in the United States.

C.ᵍⁱᵉ G.ᵍⁱᵉ TRANSATLANTIQUE
French Line

Hâvre, Plymouth, New-York.

Cie. Gle. Transatlantique/Hâvre, Plymouth, New-York, c. 1930

Albert Sebille (1874–1953)
Poster Photo Archives, Posters Please, Inc., NYC

- The poster shows the arrival in New York of French Line's new, super-luxury flagship liner, the SS *Île de France*, which had been completed in 1927. Unlike earlier passenger ships, this vessel had markedly less space for immigrants, focusing instead on a very large first-class section.

- After World War I, many shipping companies like Compagnie Générale Transatlantique, commonly known

overseas as French Line, became particularly successful, especially with American clients. Driven by an economic boom and compounded by the effects of Prohibition, wealthy Americans flocked to luxury ships with more liberal atmospheres (and plenty of alcohol). This was obviously derailed by the Great Depression.

- The perspective in this poster allows the viewer to compare the size of the ship to the recently completed Barclay-Vesey Building, one of the first Art Deco skyscrapers in New York. At the time of construction, the building was on the waterfront, however, today, its location at 140 West Street is two blocks inland due to the landfill created in 1976 to accommodate the new Battery Park City.

Cie. Gle. Transatlantique/ French Line/SS "Paris," c. 1930

Albert Sebille (1874–1953)
Image Courtesy of Alessandro Bellenda / Galleria L'Image, Alassio - Italy

- While Albert Sebille was primarily known as a painter of maritime scenes, he also created a number of posters for French Line. His signature is usually followed by an anchor, signifying that he had been appointed the coveted honor of the official painter of the French navy.

- The SS *Paris* was nicknamed the "Aristocrat of the Atlantic" due to its luxurious fittings and service. Although the ship was launched in September 1916, World War I delayed its maiden voyage until 1921.

- At the lower right of the poster, French Line boasts the measurements of the length, displacement, and power of the ship, indicating that it could easily cope with the visibly choppy waters of the Atlantic as it steamed away from New York City. The promise of a smooth journey was a key selling point in the maritime company's efforts to assuage the fears of nervous travelers.

Cunard/USA & Canada, c. 1930

Frank H. Mason (1876–1965)
Archivart / Alamy Stock Photo

- Samuel Cunard, the founder of the eponymous shipping line, had first attempted to establish the company in his hometown of Halifax, Nova Scotia. When he was unable to obtain financing there, he relocated to London, partnering with two other investors to create the company's first headquarters

in Glasgow. Cunard's first transatlantic crossing took place in 1840.

- In 1930, the now aging *Mauritania*—shown in this poster—ceased traversing the transatlantic routes and ran six-day cruises from New York to Halifax. This poster shows the liner steaming away from a stylized Lower Manhattan, its scale distorted so that the island appears to rise more steeply than it actually does.

- Frank H. Mason was a cadet in the Royal Navy and became a war artist during World War I. Much of his work from that time is housed in the Imperial War Museums. After the war, he produced posters for several shipping lines as well as the London and North Eastern Railway.

Holland-America Line, c. 1930

Designer Unknown
Image Courtesy of Poster Connection

- This unusual design focuses on New York City as a gateway to New York state and the rest of North America, showing the Erie Canal and the Great Lakes in a foreshortened perspective as the city's hinterland.

- Printed in both English and German, the composition shows the SS *Volendam*, a passenger ship operated by Holland-America Line that ran the Rotterdam–New York and Rotterdam–Halifax routes. Next to the colossal ship is a detailed rendering of the Statue of Liberty on its base designed by Richard Morris Hunt at Fort Hood.

- Holland-America Line was founded in 1873 and served as both a passenger service for immigrants as well as a luxury liner for wealthy travelers. In 2023, in acknowledgment of its long tradition of poster advertising, the company announced a poster competition to celebrate its 150th anniversary.

French Line C.G.T.
CHAMPLAIN
LAFAYETTE
ECONOMY - SHIPS THAT SET A STANDARD
"PARIS"
"LAFAYETTE"
"CHAMPLAIN"
TO
NEW YORK

French Line/New York, c. 1932

Harry Hudson Rodmell (1896–1984)
WorldPhotos / Alamy Stock Photo

- Harry Hudson Rodmell was an English artist primarily known for his maritime paintings in oil. His works hang in various maritime museums in the United Kingdom, especially in major port cities like London, Liverpool, and Hull.

- In this poster, Rodmell adapts his painterly style to a more graphically driven presentation, incorporating the French national flag as the backdrop for the two French Line ships set against the New York skyline.

- While French Line historically specialized in luxury liners, its business was negatively affected by the Great Depression and the consequent reduction in numbers of tourists. The company was bailed out by the French government and added a focus on lower-fare passengers. This poster emphasizes that French Line's new economy service, also known as third class, is still of the highest quality.

- While similar in appearance, the SS *Champlain* and the SS *Lafayette* shown in this poster had very different histories. The *Lafayette* (in the background) made her maiden voyage in 1928. Its brief but successful career was cut short when it was destroyed in a fire during a routine overhaul in 1938. The *Champlain*, shown in the foreground, was built in 1932, and was sunk by a mine off the coast of France in 1940. It was one of the first passenger ships to be lost during World War II.

To Europe the American Way/ United States Lines, 1933

Designer Unknown
Hi-Story / Alamy Stock Photo

- United States Lines had an unusual beginning. It was created in 1917 to operate German liners seized by the United States during World War I. After the war, it continued to control those ships that had been kept by the United States as reparations.

- Throughout Prohibition, the company struggled to compete with European lines on the transatlantic routes since European vessels could serve alcohol to their passengers as soon as they left US waters. As American carriers, United States Lines's ships were required to be dry.

- This poster announces the latest vessels in United States Lines's fleet. In 1932, the SS *Manhattan* was the first ship actually built for the company, at a cost of $21 million. The SS *Washington* was completed the following year.

- While the New York skyline is mostly abstract in this poster, two silhouettes on the far left can be identified as the Singer Tower and the Empire State Building.

See America
this year!
Cunard White Star

French Line C.G.T.

SOUTHAMPTON TO NEW YORK

EXPRESS LUXURY SERVICE

"ILE DE FRANCE" "NORMANDIE"

ENQUIRE WITHIN

PRINTED IN ENGLAND

OPPOSITE

**See America this Year!/
Cunard White Star**, c. 1935

Designer Unknown
*Poster House Permanent Collection
Image Courtesy of Poster House*

- This poster shows the RMS *Majestic* sailing into New York toward the Hudson River. Pier 54 at Fourteenth Street, where the ship docked, is visible in the distance.

- The composition represents one of the earliest uses of photography in a travel poster promoting New York as a destination.

- As the Cunard Line and the White Star Line merged in 1934, and the RMS *Majestic* took its final crossing on February 13, 1936, this poster is a record of a very small period of time in the history of these shipping companies.

ABOVE

**French Line/Southampton
to New York**, 1935

Designer Unknown
*Poster House Permanent Collection
Image Courtesy of Poster House*

- Launched in 1935, the SS *Normandie* was one of the most elegant ships ever to sail. Its interiors exemplified the finest French craftsmanship of the era, reflecting the prevailing Art Deco style. It also captured the Blue Riband—an unofficial award allocated for the fastest crossing of the Atlantic by a passenger ship—on its maiden voyage, making it the most expedient and efficient liner of its time.

- This poster is based on one of the many aerial photographs taken on June 3, 1935, of the *Normandie* sailing up the Hudson River along Manhattan's West Side to its berth at Pier 88 at Fifty-Fifth Street. In celebration of its much-heralded arrival, it was accompanied by tugboats and followed by steamers, ferries, and other smaller vessels.

- French Line originally used Pier 57 at Fifteenth Street as its main berth, but the era of the superliner in the 1930s required the city to build extra-long docks to safely accommodate ships like the *Queen Mary*, the *Normandie*, and the *Queen Elizabeth*. Constructed by the Public Works Administration, the special dock, one thousand feet in length, was chiseled from the schist along the coastline of Manhattan.

- Upon the outbreak of World War II, the *Normandie* was interned at her berth in New York by the United States government and ultimately seized as enemy property in 1940 when Germany invaded France. On February 9, 1942, as the *Normandie* was being converted into a troop transport ship, it caught fire and sank.

Cunard White Star

Cunard White Star, c. 1937

Tom Curr (1887–1958)
Poster House Permanent Collection
Image Courtesy of Poster House

- This poster shows the RMS *Queen Mary* steaming up the Hudson River past the lower tip of Manhattan as it is escorted by tugboats to its berth at Pier 92, located at Fiftieth Street.

- Visible within the packed cityscape of Lower Manhattan are the Whitehall Building, the City Bank–Farmers Trust Building, the Standard Oil Building, the Bank of Manhattan Trust Building, and the Cities Service Building.

- In 1934, after the Great Depression had affected transatlantic travel and all but halted ship production in Great Britain, Cunard and White Star merged to form Cunard-White Star Line. This corporate union allowed for the completion of the RMS *Queen Mary* in 1936, one of the most famous ocean liners of the period.

- The *Queen Mary*'s maiden voyage began on May 27, 1936, and for the next three years it crossed the Atlantic just under fifty times until the outbreak of World War II. In March of 1940, it sailed to Australia to be retrofitted as a troop transport, resuming commercial passenger service on July 25, 1947.

- After its final voyage in 1967, it was permanently moored in Long Beach, California, where it still serves as a floating hotel and museum.

OPPOSITE

Cunard White Star, 1938

Robert Roquin (Dates Unknown)
Image Courtesy of Swann Auction Galleries

- After the forced merger of the Cunard and White Star lines in 1934 as a result of the Great Depression, individual ships flew the flag of the original owner over the other. In this poster, the Cunard flag is displayed above the White Star burgee, indicating the origins of the ship.

- Here, Robert Roquin combines graphic design with black-and-white photography in a process known as photomontage. Originally used in various avant-garde images, the incorporation of photography into commercial advertising was fairly new at this time. The poster shows the RMS *Mauretania*, launched in 1938, against the Lower Manhattan skyline as seen from the Hudson River just north of the southern tip of the island. The blank rectangle overlapping the image would have been used for promotional text, listing the various ships and their departure dates from the United States.

- Visible at the waterline (from right to left) are the US Custom House and the New York Produce Exchange—both on Bowling Green—as well as half a dozen other buildings that are still standing today. In the background (from right to left) are the City Bank–Farmers Trust Building (with the Standard Oil Building in front of it), the Cities Service Building, the Manhattan Company Building, and, on the far left, the partially visible Singer Tower.

CUNARD WHITE STAR

CUNARD WHITE STAR

Cunard White Star, 1939

Robert Roquin (Dates Unknown)
*Image Courtesy of Swann
Auction Galleries*

- This poster shows the majestic RMS
Queen Mary and the RMS *Queen
Elizabeth* steaming away from
Manhattan toward the Atlantic with the
Chrysler Building emerging from the
skyline behind them. To its left is the
Chanin Building, while the shorter struc-
ture on its right is the New York Central

Building (known today as the Helmsley
Building) that straddles Park Avenue at
Forty-Fifth Street.

- There is an elegiac quality to the image,
which reflects a prewar optimism rather
than the brutal reality of the time. In
1940, under the direction of Winston
Churchill, Cunard sent the *Queen
Elizabeth* on its first and only journey
to New York. In an effort to escape the
Blitz, it sailed there with no passengers
and was painted in battleship gray
before returning to the fray.

- Both ships were used to transport
Allied troops during the war. Despite
the company's claim that it provided
the fastest ocean service in the world,
the *Queen Elizabeth* never actually
vied for the prize because the chairman
of Cunard did not want the ship to
compete against the *Queen Mary*. After
the war and their subsequent refur-
bishment, the ships eventually ran a
transatlantic service in tandem.

Bremen-New York, 1939

Willy Hanke (1866–1953)
Poster Photo Archives, Posters Please, Inc., NYC

- This Art Deco–style poster, with its dramatic and unexpected color scheme, promotes Norddeutscher Lloyd's passenger service from Bremen, Germany, to New York City. It is one of the last advertisements made for the company.

- Before the outbreak of World War II, the shipping company owned seventy vessels. That entire fleet was either destroyed during the war or given to the Allies as reparations. Of the three ships shown in this poster, the SS *Columbus* was sunk in 1939, the SS *Bremen* burned in 1941, and the SS *Europa* became the SS *Liberté* after it was claimed by France in 1947.

- Of the various stylized Art Deco towers rising above the ships in the background, the Empire State Building is the most notable, literally extending above the clouds.

- Wilhelm Hanken was a maritime oil painter who used the name Willy Hanke on commercial work produced for Norddeutscher Lloyd, Cunard, and Deutsche Lufthansa.

ABOVE

**Saturnia-Vulcania/
Per New York**, 1948

Giovanni Patrone (1904–63)
*Image Courtesy of Alessandro Bellenda /
Galleria L'Image, Alassio - Italy*

- The poster was printed to herald the
return of Italian Line's service from
Genoa to New York after World War
II. In 1947, the MS *Saturnia* made the
journey first, with its sister ship, the
MS *Vulcania*, following a year later. The
iconic New York symbols of the Chrysler
and Empire State Buildings can be seen
emerging from the yellow haze in the
background.

- Both ships were launched in a blaze
of publicity, with advertising designed
by celebrated artists like Argio Orell.
Commissioned by Cosulich Line (one
of the eight companies that merged to
become Italian Line), they were among
the first liners to feature diesel engines.

- The *Saturnia* and the *Vulcania* were the
longest-serving passenger liners that
had been constructed during the 1920s.
When, in April 1965, they departed New
York for the last time, maritime reporter
Werner Bamberger published a eulogy
for them in the *New York Times*.

OPPOSITE

Home Lines/Italia, 1949

Mario Puppo (1905–77)
*Image Courtesy of Alessandro Bellenda /
Galleria L'Image, Alassio - Italy*

- Created in the aftermath of World War
II, Home Lines was a shipping company
born out of a partnership among a
handful of corporations, with Swedish
American Line and Cosulich Lines of
Trieste having majority shares.

- This poster announces the company's
first voyage from Genoa to New York via
Naples and Lisbon. Previously, Home
Lines had focused on the Genoa–South

America route. It shows the *Italia* (originally MS *Kungsholm* under Swedish
American Line), which had been used
by the United States to transport troops
under the name *John Ericsson*.

- By emphasizing the geometry of the
city's skyscrapers as vertical lines
crowned by the night sky, Mario Puppo
cleverly evokes the stars and stripes of
the American flag.

CUNARD

CHERBOURG — NEW YORK

"QUEEN ELIZABETH" — "QUEEN MARY"

Cunard/Cherbourg–New York, c. 1950

Designer Unknown
Poster Photo Archives, Posters Please, Inc., NYC

- Although the Cunard-White Star Line was formed as a merger between the two companies in response to the financial difficulties they experienced during the Great Depression, by 1947, Cunard was so successful that it bought White Star's shares. In 1950, it reverted to the name of Cunard and launched the long-planned two-ship, weekly service to New York from Southampton in England, with a stopover in Cherbourg, France.

- After serving as troop carriers during World War II, both the RMS *Queen Mary* and the RMS *Queen Elizabeth* had to be refitted and furnished as passenger liners. Despite six years of war service, the *Queen Elizabeth* had never undertaken the regulation sea trials required to prove the ship was seaworthy for commercial use. When the time came, Queen Elizabeth and her daughters, Princess Elizabeth and Princess Margaret, rode aboard the *Queen Elizabeth* during its trials.

- This poster features the dramatic skyline of Lower Manhattan and the Financial District, with the rather less-imposing docks in Cherbourg, France, the port of origin, appearing opposite.

French Line/To and From Europe, c. 1950

Mimouca Nebel (Dates Unknown)
*Poster House Permanent Collection
Image Courtesy of Poster House*

- After World War II, Germany was required to give members of the Allied nations many of its vessels as part of the reparations agreement. The SS *Europa* had been owned by Norddeutscher Lloyd Bremen and was given to French Line, which renamed it the SS *Liberté*. From August 1950, this became the company's flagship vessel. This poster was one of the first to feature the *Liberté* as part of French Line's fleet.

- Reminiscent of a watercolor painting, this evocative composition shows a bird's-eye view of Lower Manhattan, looking south past the silhouette of the Empire State Building. In the distance, the *Liberté* floats up the Hudson River in the direction of Pier 57 at Fifteenth Street, where the Compagnie Générale Transatlantique (French Line) had its terminal.

- This design is distinguished from other posters advertising New York City since it features three distinctly old-fashioned buildings among the modern skyscrapers in downtown: the tower of the Municipal Building, the dome of the Sohmer Piano Building, and the Metropolitan Life Insurance Company Tower.

To and From EUROPE

French Line

NEW YORK

SWISSAIR

New York/Swissair, 1951

Henri Ott (1919–2009)
Poster House Permanent Collection
Image Courtesy of Poster House

- Henri Ott created more than twenty designs for Swissair promoting various destinations, all of them in linocut. Also known as linoleum printing, the process is similar to woodcut in which a design is carved or cut into a surface, creating raised lines that can then be printed.

- Here, the artist presents a romanticized view of Manhattan, seen from the East River on a tugboat as it passes under the Brooklyn Bridge at sunrise. This type of view—a gritty, everyday snapshot of the fringes of modern life in the big city—was represented by many Depression-era artists and reflected the influence of their immediate predecessors in the Ashcan School. As such, it is one of the earliest posters that describes a specific atmosphere rather than displaying the technological marvels of the massive metropolis.

Farrell Lines/Wonderful way to get there..., c. 1951

Frederick "Fritz" Siebel (1913–91)
Collection of Jolean & David Breger
Image Courtesy of Poster House

- In 1948, American South African Lines was renamed Farrell Lines, providing passenger and cargo service between South Africa and New York. By the early 1950s, two single-funnel sister ships—the *African Enterprise* and the *African Endeavor*—plied the route between Cape Town and Manhattan. The all-first-class vessels were equipped to carry eighty-two passengers each. It is not clear which of the two ships is depicted in this poster.

- To promote travel to New York City, Frederick Siebel created an imaginary, collaged cityscape and urban portrait, incorporating iconic monuments, buildings, and neighborhoods like the Brooklyn Bridge, the United Nations, and Times Square. In vibrant, stained-glass tones he showcases the city simultaneously dappled in sun and lit up at night.

105

New York
par la "TRANSAT"

COMPAGNIE GENERALE TRANSATLANTIQUE

NEW YORK
AMERICAN AIRLINES

New York par la "Transat,"
c. 1955

Albert Brenet (1903–2005)
Private Collection, New York
Image Courtesy of Poster House

- This is one of the few posters that highlights the legacy of Manhattan's commercial shipping industry, focusing on the myriad docks and boats that populated the East River.

- Looking south from the Manhattan Bridge, the viewer's eye travels along FDR Drive as it sweeps beneath the Brooklyn Bridge toward the Financial District. Meanwhile, the Brooklyn Bridge, the City Bank–Farmers Trust Building, the Cities Service Building, and the Manhattan Company Building dominate the skyline. At the far right can be seen a small section of the recently completed Alfred E. Smith Houses.

- Manhattan's prominence as a commercial port ended in the early 1950s. In 1951, Port Newark in New Jersey had modernized, quickly surpassing New York in popularity due to its easy access to rail lines and highways, along with ample room for cranes and hoists to load and unload ships. By the mid-1950s, shipping companies had almost fully migrated to the Garden State.

New York/American Airlines,
c. 1960

Designer Unknown
Image Courtesy of Illustration Gallery

- While at first glance this composition may appear to be based on photographs, it is actually derived from a detailed oil painting of two New York scenes. Above, a ferry glides across Upper New York Bay, while below, a tugboat passes against the misty skyline of Lower Manhattan.

- While tugboats were ubiquitous along the Hudson River in the nineteenth and early twentieth centuries, by the 1960s they were rarely seen. This poster thus combines nostalgia with the contemporary cityscape to promote air travel to New York.

NEW YORK

ss ARGENTINA · ss BRASIL
MOORE-McCORMACK LINES

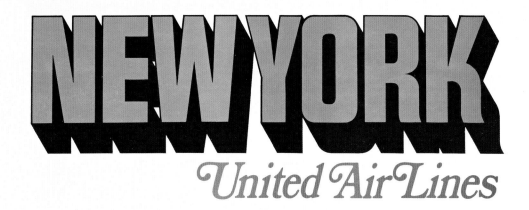

NEW YORK
United Air Lines

OPPOSITE

New York/Moore-McCormack Lines, 1964

Designer Unknown
Image Courtesy of Affiche Passion

- Moore-McCormack Lines was primarily a freight shipping company based out of New York City. Founded in 1913, it slowly added various vessels to its fleet, consolidating numerous companies under one banner just before World War II.

- This anonymously designed poster promotes passenger travel aboard the newly renovated SS *Argentina* and SS *Brasil* that sailed the New York–to–South America route from 1958 to 1969. A few years after it was published, however, declining passenger numbers caused the company to discontinue its service.

- The poster proved so popular that it was also used as a magazine advertisement for the company in 1965, promoting a number of destinations, including Africa and the Caribbean.

RIGHT

New York/United Air Lines, 1967

James Jebary (Dates Unknown)
Poster House Permanent Collection
Image Courtesy of Poster House

- James Jebary was a prolific designer for United Airlines in the late 1960s, producing posters in his trademark pop-influenced style for domestic destinations.

- Although not as iconic as New York's skyscrapers, ferries are omnipresent on New York City's waterways. Here, Jebary depicts a colorful interpretation of the Staten Island Ferry, part of the busiest ferry route in the United States.

PRINTED IN U.S.A.

Compagni-e Générale Transatlantique/SS France, 1968

John Bainbridge (1918–78)
Poster Photo Archives, Posters Please, Inc., NYC

- The SS *France* was the flagship of the French Line. France was especially proud of the quality of its passenger ships throughout the twentieth century and often used them as a type of soft power—at the time of its maiden voyage in 1960, the *France* was the longest ship ever built.

- The construction of the *France* was controversial as it was publicly funded and pushed through by the country's autocratic president, Charles de Gaulle. To defray costs, it functioned as both a transatlantic liner that made direct crossings as well as a cruise ship that took more circuitous journeys.

- The Australian-born designer John Bainbridge created a unique conceit when designing this poster. Rather than show the skyline or an image of the boat, he set one of the ship's distinctive flying fin funnels against a Cubist inter-pretation of New York City's skyscrapers, merging the elements on overlapping planes. It is an abstract yet evocative advertisement for travel to New York.

THE NEW YORK WORLD'S FAIRS

New York was host to two world's fairs in the twentieth century. The 1939 New York World's Fair was the largest single event in the United States before World War II. Marketed around the world, the fair was enormously popular and received approximately forty-four million visitors during its two-year run. Planned during the Great Depression, it was intended to help lift the city's struggling economy while encouraging public optimism for the future with its theme of "The World of Tomorrow." Television was among the many futuristic novelties presented to the world at the fair, with RCA broadcasting the opening ceremony in the first scheduled television transmission in the United States. In 1964, another world's fair was held on the same grounds in Queens.

OPPOSITE

New York/Holland-America Line, 1938

Willem Frederick ten Broek (1905–93)
Collection of William W. Crouse
Image Courtesy of Poster House

- For all the great domestic graphic advertising produced for the 1939 New York World's Fair, some of the best and rarest images were designed by foreign shipping lines. Both the Cunard-White Star Line and the Holland America Line created posters promoting their passenger service to the event. Unlike American posters, they not only show the Trylon and Perisphere, but also use stylized Art Deco renderings of New York's skyline to entice clients. Many posters like this were printed in multiple languages to reach a broad audience.

- Here, the elegant *Nieuw Amsterdam* is shown steaming into New York, the smoothness of the crossing suggested by the unmoving reflection in the water of the Trylon and Perisphere. The ship's original name was the *Prinsendam*, but it was changed to *Nieuw Amsterdam* to honor the original Dutch name of New York City.

- It is not certain how often Holland America Line actually offered this world's fair service, as the *Nieuw Amsterdam* only made seventeen transatlantic crossings after its maiden voyage in 1938, many of which predate the opening of the fair. After the outbreak of World War II in 1939—just four months after the fair began—the ship stopped transatlantic service and was briefly used to cruise to the Caribbean. When the Netherlands fell to Germany in May 1940, the vessel was taken over by the British Ministry of War Transport and converted to a troop ship. It began to offer passenger service again in October 1947.

NEW YORK

EXPOSITION MONDIALE

EXCURSIONS PAR

HOLLAND-AMERICA LINE

NEW YORK WORLD'S FAIR
THE WORLD OF TOMORROW 1939

**New York World's Fair:
The World of Tomorrow**, 1939

Joseph Binder (1898–1972)
Collection of William W. Crouse
Image Courtesy of Poster House

- In a visualization of "The World of Tomorrow," Joseph Binder boldly depicts the Trylon and Perisphere, the two largest structures built for the 1939 world's fair. Designed by architects J. André Fouilhoux and Wallace Harrison, they were known collectively as the Theme Center and appeared on almost all promotional items for the event.

- The lower half of the poster focuses on the transport of residents of the world at large to the fair, showing a train arriving from an overnight journey and a ship making its way across the Atlantic, both in the direction of the illuminated skyline of Manhattan.

- Binder's composition is one of the finest examples of American Art Deco graphic design. Despite his fame as a designer, he was not originally commissioned to create the poster; instead, he submitted this image to a competition for the world's fair in 1938 and won first prize.

**Pennsylvania Railroad/
World's Fair**, 1939

Sascha Maurer (1897–1961)
Poster House Permanent Collection
Image Courtesy of Poster House

- The Long Island Railroad—a subsidiary of the Pennsylvania Railroad—built a new world's fair station along its existing tracks in Flushing, Queens. The ultramodern station, which reflected "The World of Tomorrow" theme, can be seen here in the distance near the Trylon and Perisphere.

- The foreground of the composition shows the original Pennsylvania Station next to a stylized version of the Manhattan skyline. The train tracks cutting through the city emphasize the "Direct Route" from Midtown to the fair, a tagline that was included in all advertising for the event. These rides were also promoted as costing only ten cents for the ten-minute journey.

- Sascha Maurer was born in Germany and studied under the famous poster designer Ludwig Hohlwein. After World War I, he emigrated to Brazil and then the United States. He became a prominent graphic designer who worked for several major East Coast railroad companies, among them the New York Central Line, the Pennsylvania Railroad, and the New Haven Railroad. This is one of three images he created for the 1939 New York World's Fair.

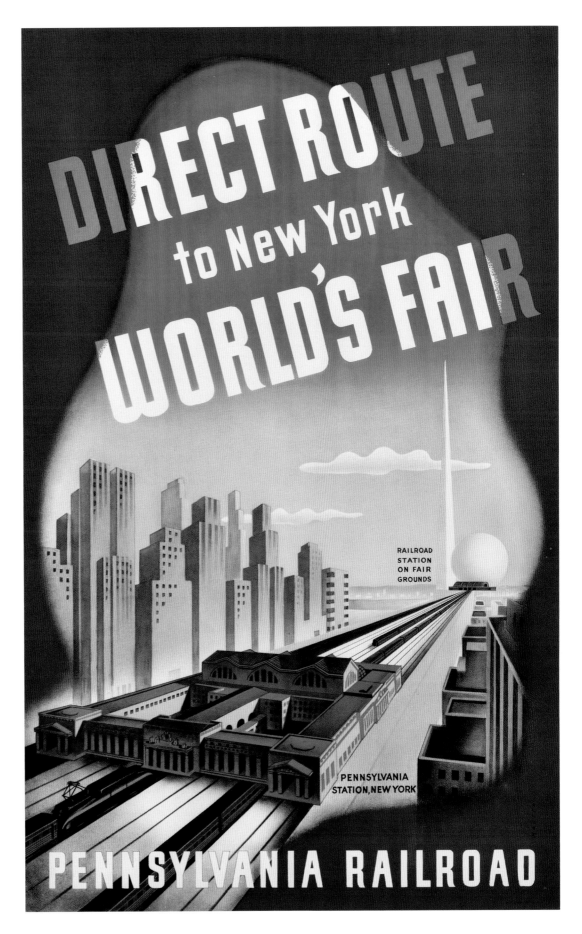

Pennsylvania Railroad/World's Fair New York, 1939

Sascha Maurer (1897–1961)
Image Courtesy of Swann Auction Galleries

- Here, Sascha Maurer promotes the Pennsylvania Railroad's specialty service to the World's Fair by emphasizing its convenient location next to the New York Subway system and the temporary purpose-built route to the fairgrounds. It was thus the ideal means of traveling to the city for the event.

- Maurer's design for this poster echoes the glamorous ski posters that defined his advertising career, with large, elegant figures in the foreground gazing at an alluring backdrop.

- During the heyday of American rail travel in the 1920s and '30s, competitive advertising between railroads was commonplace. The Pennsylvania Railroad often claimed that it had the shortest route between west and east, with the heaviest rail and finest roadbed in the country.

General Motors/New York World's Fair, 1939

Designer Unknown
Image Courtesy of Swann Auction Galleries

- General Motors's 35,738-square-foot "Highways and Horizons" pavilion at the 1939 World's Fair contained *Futurama*, the event's most popular exhibit. Designed by Norman Bel Geddes, the eighteen-minute ride transported visitors in moving sound chairs along a conveyor. The experience is represented in this poster through a combination of graphic design and photomontage, in which illustrated participants travel through prophetic images of America twenty years in the future, centered around the car and massive highways.

- For those unable to attend the World's Fair, GM produced a twenty-three-minute film, *To New Horizons*, that looks ahead to the "wonder world of 1960."

- The film opens with the line "In a restless search for new opportunities and new ways of living," one that effectively summarizes the relentless optimism of the American Century, the era in which the United States increasingly became the dominant global economic power.

- The poster also lists a variety of well-known GM brands, including Buick, Chevrolet, and Frigidaire, which the company owned from 1919 to 1979.

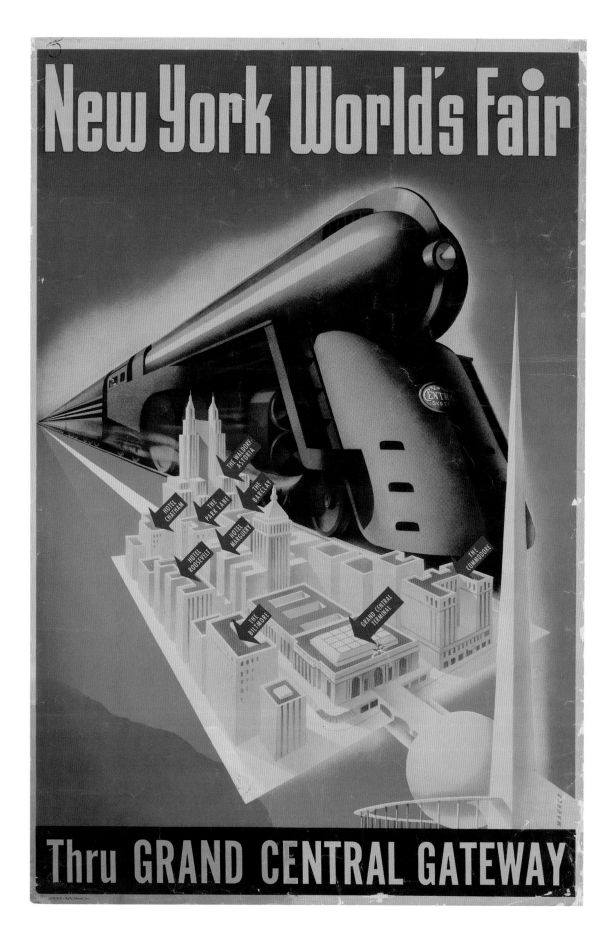

New York World's Fair, c. 1939

Sascha Maurer (1897–1961)
*Image Courtesy of Swann
Auction Galleries*

- The centerpiece of this image is the iconic 20th Century Limited train, designed by Henry Dreyfuss. It ran between New York and Chicago from 1938 to 1968. Next to it is a three-dimensional model of Terminal City, the complex of buildings above the train yard of Grand Central—hence the caption "Thru Grand Central Gateway."

- In order to both encourage and handle increased numbers of visitors to the world's fair, a special spur of the Independent Subway System in New York was constructed. The extension cost a staggering $1.7 million (roughly $37 million today), and riders were therefore charged double the typical five-cent subway fare to get to the fairgrounds. The dedicated train line was not a great success, however, and ultimately carried only 54 percent of the projected number of passengers. It was demolished in 1941, just a few months after the world's fair ended.

New York World's Fair/Cunard White Star, c. 1939

Janno (Dates Unknown)
Image Courtesy of Poster Connection

- As it faced severe financial trouble during the Great Depression, the British government backed the merger of Cunard and White Star, provided that they combined their North Atlantic operations. Here, its special service to the New York World's Fair is announced in a stylized Art Deco design on a silver metallic background.

- The poster depicts a condensed version of the city's skyline, positioning the actual fair near the waterfront of Lower Manhattan rather than in its actual location in Queens, which could not be reached from the sea.

PEACE AND FREEDOM

WORLD'S FAIR OF 1940 IN NEW YORK

World's Fair of 1940 in New York, 1940

Designer Unknown
Image Courtesy of Swann Auction Galleries

- Built on a former ash dump, the world's fair literally rose like a phoenix onto the Queens landscape, covering 1,216 acres.

- This poster, published for the fair's second year, provides a well-manicured view of Fountain Lake, with the Perisphere and Trylon in the background. These two monumental structures were intended to evoke an optimistic, technologically progressive future. The Perisphere was 180 feet in diameter, connected to the

610-foot-high spire of the Trylon by what was then the world's longest escalator.

- The Perisphere housed *Democracity*, a diorama designed by Henry Dreyfuss that depicted a utopian city of the future.

**American Airlines/
New York World's Fair**, 1961

Henry K. Bencsath (1909–96)
*Poster House Permanent Collection
Image Courtesy of Poster House*

- The Unisphere in Flushing Meadows Corona Park, now a New York City landmark, was designed by Gilmore

D. Clarke as part of the 1964 New York World's Fair. Built on the footprint of the Perisphere from the 1939 World's Fair, the steel Unisphere is 140 feet high and weighs 900,000 pounds.

- This structure was chosen as the emblem for the fair, representing the theme "Peace Through Understanding" and celebrating the beginning of the Space

Age. Its three orbital rings are intended to signify the first man-made satellites.

- While the poster advertises American Airlines's service to the fair, US Steel paid for the construction of the Unisphere in exchange for publicity. Its name appears in small print at the lower right corner of this poster.

- The 1964 world's fair was intended as an updated version of the 1939 event. The fair was split into five distinct areas: industrial, international, transportation, federal, and states. With the theme of "Peace Through Understanding" in the wake of the Cuban Missile Crisis, it showcased American technology and culture.

- The Maharaja—the iconic mascot of Air-India—is shown here supporting the Unisphere, the symbol of the fair, in place of Atlas. Whether intentional or not, his pose also references one of New York's best-known sculptures, the bronze Atlas designed by Lee Lawrie and Rene Paul Chambellan in Rockefeller Center.

- The Unisphere was built from stainless steel in 110 days. At the time, it was the largest globe in the world. As part of the goal of promoting technology during the Space Age, each of its surrounding rings represents one of the three pioneering figures in interstellar flight: Yuri Gagarin, John Glenn, and the *Telstar* satellite.

- This poster for United Air Lines's service to New York City specifically promotes the company as a means of getting to the 1964 world's fair. A diagrammatic view of the fairgrounds in Flushing Meadows Corona Park in Queens dominates much of the image behind the plane's tail fin, emphasizing their great scale. The poster does not, however, advertise a key selling point: the park was less than four miles from LaGuardia Airport. A new Central Terminal Building was completed there just in time for the fair, with United initiating flights to the airport from Chicago and Cleveland.

- Even with exceptional promotion and high-quality exhibits, it was a financial disaster; investors received an estimated return of just under twenty cents per dollar (as opposed to the forty cents per dollar return that they had made on the 1939 world's fair at the same location).

- Raymond Loewy's United logo in red, white, and blue is prominently displayed here, its patriotic colors further championing the American technological prowess represented at the fair. It also tacitly asserted the value of American capitalism over the communist ideology of the country's Soviet rivals.

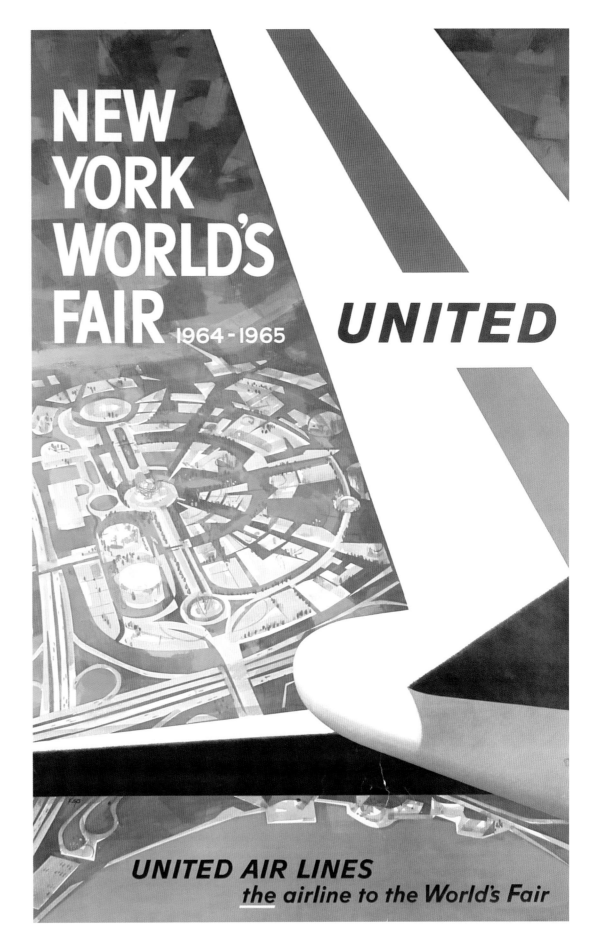

I'VE SEEN THE FUTURE: SASCHA MAURER'S POSTERS FOR THE 1939 NEW YORK WORLD'S FAIR

BY MICHELE WASHINGTON

While New York City in the 1930s was marked by the Great Depression at the beginning of the decade and the start of World War II in Europe toward its end, it nonetheless flourished. Architects designed increasingly ambitious skyscrapers, among them the Chrysler Building and the Empire State Building, that combined Art Deco facades with luxurious lobbies. During this decade, baseball, America's favorite sport, captivated New Yorkers in particular as the Yankees won five World Series in a row.

Even under Prohibition (1920–33), underground nightlife thrived in speakeasies, hidden after-hours spots offering entertainment and illegal alcohol. Jazz clubs flourished from Midtown to Harlem uptown, and the hippest musicians played syncopated rhythms alongside glamorous female jazz singers scatting lyrics. During the 1930s, the nickname the Big Apple was used by Black jazz musicians to describe New York City, and especially Harlem, as the jazz center of the world. Yet class and economic disparity separated New Yorkers, as some had the means for such amusements while others struggled to find work, shelter, and food.

Even though America was in economic turmoil during this decade, progress was still possible. In 1935, for example, the New York World's Fair Corporation was formed under the leadership of Grover Whalen with the aim of developing an exceptional event that would stimulate economic growth in New York City and beyond. Over the next four years, they planned a fair that would allow visitors a glimpse of a future fostered by scientific innovation, on the theme of "The World of Tomorrow." The organization established the World's Fair around seven thematic zones: amusement, communication, community interest, food, government, production and distribution, and transportation. Together with the World's Fair Corporation, New York City Parks Department's commissioner Robert Moses oversaw the conversion of the marshy Queens Flushing Meadows grounds into fairgrounds spanning about 1,200 acres.

Designers, illustrators, and other agencies were quickly hired to produce advertisements and campaign materials for the fair. Its seven thematic zones attracted corporations eager to promote their products, inventions, and services to American consumers—among them AT&T, General Motors, Kodak, Ford, NBC, and Westinghouse. Anyone visiting the fair would have plenty to experience, from exhibits to the pavilions and the amusement areas, all meant to entice the senses and entertain. There were exhibitors representing more than sixty countries, among them France, Greece, Japan, Italy, the USSR, and Sweden, allowing visitors to experience aspects of other cultures without traveling abroad.

One popular exhibit, *Futurama*, was created by visionary industrial designer Norman Bel Geddes and sponsored by General Motors. Visitors were transported on an aerial conveyor system over a model of scenic suburbs and superhighways, accompanied by a voice-over and sound effects. The aim was to encourage them to envisage the future of cities in twenty years as spacious places accessible by highways (very much to the advantage of General Motors). As people left the exhibit, they were given pins that said, "I have seen the future." These keepsakes were reminders of what they had just experienced and what might lie ahead.

Sascha Maurer was commissioned to design three posters for the World's Fair that would represent the commerce and transportation theme. The German-born Maurer emigrated to New York City in 1925. He worked briefly for émigré poster designer Lucian Bernhard before establishing his own studio where he designed book jackets, magazine covers, and posters. By the 1930s, Maurer was creating posters for ski resorts in New England, and these eventually caught the attention of the New Haven railroad line, where he began to illustrate travel posters. Starting in 1943, he also designed and illustrated *Ford Times*, a magazine made by the Ford Motor Company.

The New York World's Fair highlighted American innovation in industry, art, and design, reinforcing the city's primacy as the capital of culture and consumerism. Yet much of the innovation being introduced during the '30s was by the many émigrés who had arrived in New York after fleeing Fascism in Europe, among them, graphic designers like Sascha Maurer.

Maurer's posters for the World's Fair featured the Art Deco style of the new Chrysler (1930) and Empire State (1931) Buildings, as well as the neighboring major hotels. The two iconic skyscrapers in Midtown played an important role in advertising for the New York World's Fair in general. These structures, successively the tallest in the world, symbolized the modern innovation and ambition of New York City. They also reshaped the skyline that, along with the Statue of Liberty, became its most familiar emblem.

In each of his three designs for the fair, Maurer emphasized the dramatic modernism of New York City, one that corresponded to the ambitions of the event, as he addressed the commerce and transportation theme. Two of his World's Fair posters were commissioned by the Pennsylvania Railroad Company (see pages 117 and 118), both of which incorporated a view of the Manhattan skyline as well as the celebrated Trylon and Perisphere monuments that came to symbolize the fair. At that time, Manhattan was the center of New York City and Midtown was the center of Manhattan. The third poster (and probably the only one) was for the New York Central System (see page 120), featuring a model of Grand Central Terminal and its luxurious Art Deco train, the 20th Century Limited. His hand-lettered typography in this poster combined condensed sans-serif text with drop shadows, calling attention to the words. He also sometimes combined sans serif with bold script.

Like much of the promotional material for the fair, Maurer's posters featured two of its most-distinctive structures: the Trylon and Perisphere. The Trylon, a stark-white 610-foot spire that jetted upward like a spear shooting toward the heavens, was connected to the Perisphere, a gigantic orb the size of a city block. These futuristic forms were designed by architectural masterminds Wallace Harrison and J. André Fouilhoux to symbolize the fair's utopian futurism.

Visionary industrial designer Henry Dreyfuss's diorama *Democracity* was housed in the Perisphere—reflecting "The World of Tomorrow" theme. Visitors entered the Perisphere via the Helicline, a spiral, elevated walkway; there was also a slide presentation projected on the dome's surface. The Trylon and Perisphere featured not only in promotional posters for the fair but also on postage stamps, souvenirs, and signage.

Between its opening in April 1939 and its closure in October 1940, an estimated forty-five million people visited the fairgrounds in Queens, so information about public transportation was obviously important. One of Maurer's posters promoting the Pennsylvania Railroad heralds a "Direct Route to the World's Fair" with "Pennsylvania Station" and "Railroad Station on Fairgrounds" clearly marked at opposite ends of the track. In another design, Maurer fashions a nighttime scene with a couple set to travel to the fair. They eagerly look toward the grounds with beaming smiles, apparently excited about what awaits them.

In New York World's Fair for the New York Central System, Maurer shows the 20th Century Limited, the streamlined pride of the New York Central Line, as it glides into Grand Central Terminal, represented here in a small model seen from above. The station is surrounded by such swanky Midtown hotels as the Commodore, the Biltmore, the Roosevelt, the Marguery, the Park Lane, the Barclay, and the Waldorf Astoria. The model serves as a visual summary of the transportation and accommodation options available to travelers. Grand Central Terminal was then, as now, a major transportation hub between New York City; Westchester, Connecticut; and other points throughout the United States. A temporary subway line, the World's Fair Line, was constructed specially to serve the fair.

When Sascha Maurer began working as a graphic designer in the 1920s, traditional, figurative forms dominated popular imagery. However, by the end of World War II, this style had been partly superseded by the compositions from a new breed of American graphic designers who were under the influence of European modernism. This was a visual language represented in the design of the world's fair itself and its optimistic, even utopian theme of "The World of Tomorrow." (After the outbreak of war in Europe in September 1939, this was changed to "For Peace and Freedom.") In spite of its remarkable structures and products, however, the fair fell short of the one hundred million anticipated visitors, and only about forty cents of each invested dollar was recouped. Nonetheless, its innovations ultimately had a significant positive impact on the American economy, and, not least, on the development of the country's art, architecture, and design.

NEW YORK FROM THE AIR

With the emergence of transatlantic air travel after the war, airline companies began to promote different aspects of city life in their advertising. While airmail service had been introduced between Europe and South America during the 1930s, airlines only had the capacity to transport passengers across the Atlantic with the arrival of "flying boats" later that decade. Commercial flights, however, did not become commonplace until after the end of World War II. Plane travel became increasingly popular during the late 1940s, but these early flights were expensive, much like the high-priced crossings on luxury ocean liners. Graphic designers had to find novel ways to present a city whose image was already established in the public imagination. These new airline posters thus often featured aerial views and unusual perspectives.

Deutsche Zeppelin-Reederei, 1936

Jupp Wiertz (1881–1939)
Private Collection, NYC
Image Courtesy of Poster House

- This is the earliest poster promoting international air travel to New York City. It advertises a two-night crossing aboard the *Hindenburg* zeppelin from Germany, showing the skyscrapers of Lower Manhattan nearly disappearing under fog. A dramatic gap in the cloudy sky illuminates the spire of the Cities Service Building—still standing today at 70 Pine Street. Visible from left to right are the silhouettes of the Irving Trust Company Building (known today as One Wall Street) and the Manhattan Company Building at 40 Wall Street.

- Many historians have incorrectly identified the illuminated skyscraper here not as the Cities Service Building but as the Empire State Building, the most iconic structure in the city at the time. While it was under construction, there was a plan to include a dirigible docking station at the top of its tower. This idea, while excellent for marketing, was quickly abandoned as winds proved too unpredictable at 1,350 feet to safely allow passengers to disembark. Jupp Wiertz was most likely inspired by a 1936 newsreel that showed the airship soaring past these buildings.

- The *Hindenburg* made nine complete flights over the Atlantic from Germany to Lakehurst, New Jersey. On its tenth crossing on May 6, 1937, its illustrious career came to an end when it burst into flames while trying to land. The airship bore swastikas on its tail fins, emblems of the Nazi party, which frequently used dirigibles for propaganda purposes.

- This is the German-language variant of the poster. It also was issued in French, Italian, and English.

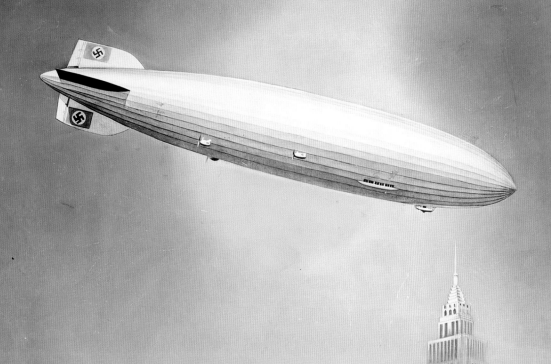

IN 2 TAGEN NACH NORD-AMERIKA!
DEUTSCHE ZEPPELIN-REEDEREI

AIR FRANCE
AMÉRIQUE DU NORD

Air France/Amérique du Nord, 1946

Guy Arnoux (1886–1951)
Private Collection, New York
Image Courtesy of Poster House

- On July 1, 1946, Air France began offering direct flights to New York. Here, Guy Arnoux represents North America with a proverbial "city in the clouds" set against a patriotic stars-and-stripes sky. As in so many earlier posters, New York City serves as visual shorthand for the entire country.

- Arnoux's abstract rendering of Manhattan combines skyscrapers with earlier architectural elements like chimneys and water tanks. The curved structure on the left is most likely one of the massive lunette windows in the original Pennsylvania Station or the arc of the Hell Gate Bridge over the East River.

- Air France acquired its first Lockheed Constellation in 1946. In anticipation of its regular service, which did not begin until 1947, Arnoux included an image of one at the upper right of the poster. These propeller-driven, four-engine planes were the first pressurized cabin aircraft to be widely used for commercial travel, greatly improving the quality and safety of flights. From Paris to New York, the journey took twenty hours and required one stop, in Gander, Newfoundland, for refueling.

TWA/Etats-Unis, c. 1947

Frank Soltesz (1912–86)
Poster House Permanent Collection
Image Courtesy of Poster House

- This poster depicts a Connie on its final descent into New York City's LaGuardia Airport. The airline would ultimately operate out of Idlewild Airport (later known as John F. Kennedy Airport) in 1949.

- TWA began its postwar operations in early 1946, with a fleet of ten Lockheed Constellations (familiarly known as "Connies"). Its logo featuring an arrow piercing the company's initials was in use through 1947 but continued to appear in advertisements until the following year.

- This poster proved so popular that multiple variants, incorporating distinctive colored borders and text, were published into the 1950s. This version was intended for the French market and boasts some of the airline's new destinations—the Middle East, India, Africa, Europe, and the United States—with a sweeping view of Manhattan standing in for all of them. It was in circulation between 1946 and 1948.

ETATS-UNIS EUROPE
MOYEN ORIENT INDE AFRIQUE

TWA

TRANS WORLD AIRLINE

AMÉRIQUE DU NORD

AIR FRANCE

Air France/Amérique du Nord,
1948

Luc-Marie Bayle (1914–2000)
Image Courtesy of Poster Connection

- Although this poster is notionally meant to promote travel from France to North America, it actually represents some of the marvels of Paris and New York City, joining the Brooklyn Bridge with the Pont Neuf, and the Eiffel Tower, the Arc de Triomphe, and the Sacré-Coeur alongside various Manhattan skyscrapers. The Statue of Liberty acts as a unifying visual motif at the center of the scene, an acknowledgment of France's long-standing history with (and generosity toward) the United States.

- Interestingly, the Eiffel Tower is shown as being the same height as the Empire State Building, despite being more than 250 feet shorter.

- A Lockheed Constellation is shown at the upper right; this aircraft flew the transatlantic route for Air France before the dawn of the Jet Age, stopping at Shannon, Ireland, and Gander, Newfoundland.

- Luc-Marie Bayle was most famous for his watercolor paintings, particularly of maritime subjects. The image of an anchor next to his signature indicates that he was an official painter of the French navy. He was also the director of the Musée Nationale de la Marine in Paris.

American Airlines to New York,
1948

Edward McKnight Kauffer (1890–1954)
The Merrill C. Berman Collection
Image Courtesy of Poster House

- After designing legendary posters for the London Underground during the 1920s and '30s, American artist Edward McKnight Kauffer moved back to the United States from England, bringing with him a European modernist approach to poster design that the *New York Times* described as "intellectually dynamic."

- While Kauffer saw New York City as a "depressing canyon of mortar, steel, bricks and glass [compared to London]," he understood the special qualities that the metropolis lent to advertising. This is one of the few posters of the period that presents the city from below, as someone on the street would see it, constantly forced to look up—making it a figurative allegory of postwar optimism.

- While Kauffer was familiar with European tastes, this poster is aimed specifically at an American audience. Until 1950, American Airlines was a national carrier—a subsidiary known as American Overseas Airlines flew the Atlantic from 1945 to 1950.

AMERICAN AIRLINES

 TO NEW YORK

E. Mcknight Kauffer

American Airlines to New York, c. 1948

Edward McKnight Kauffer (1890–1954)
Private Collection, New York
Image Courtesy of Poster House

- Kauffer was struck by the contradiction between the pace of life in New York City and the static prettiness of posters promoting it as a destination. In 1921, he wrote that the business of advertising was to reflect the actual urban experience; an encounter with a poster on the street should feel as real as seeing a fire engine at speed. He attempted to embrace this concept in his graphic designs, an approach that set his work apart from that of his colleagues in America.

- This avant-garde composition is the first promoting New York City to incorporate photo collage. In it, a Douglas DC-6, first used by American Airlines late in 1946, soars over the cityscape and a prominent, golden version of the Statue of Liberty. The exceptional use of white space and collaged photo elements would have been seen as incredibly radical at the time.

Swissair/USA, 1949

Henri Ott (1919–2009)
Private Collection, New York
Image Courtesy of Poster House

- Designed for a Swiss audience, this dynamic photo-collage poster combines disparate New York City landmarks, including part of the Brooklyn Bridge; the view of Manhattan's West Side from the Hudson River, including the freight and passenger ferry terminals of the Lackawanna and the Central Railroad of New Jersey, respectively; and an unusual, aerial view of two of the main buildings at Rockefeller Center.

- The predominance of the red, white, and blue of the American flag reflects the tradition of using New York City to represent all of the United States.

- This poster is from the inaugural year of Swissair's service to America, a fairly avant-garde choice for a company wanting to introduce its New York service to its passengers.

New York by Clipper/Pan American World Airlines, 1950

Designer Unknown
Collection Galerie 1 2 3 - Geneva/
Switzerland
www.galerie123.com

- Before 1958, when the first generation of jet planes began to offer transatlantic service, there was a running battle between airlines attempting to fly across the ocean with the fewest stops. Although strong tailwinds made it possible for many planes to fly a nonstop eastward journey from New York to Europe, headwinds on the return trip required at least one stop in Gander, Newfoundland.

- The airport in Gander became famous once again following the terrorist attacks of September 11, 2001, when thirty-eight planes carrying seven thousand passengers were ordered to land there as US airspace was closed.

- This poster features a Boeing 377 Stratocruiser, a double-decker plane used only by Pan Am, BOAC (British Overseas Airways Corporation), and American Overseas Airlines for transatlantic flights. Since it was derived from a long-range bomber, for the time it had an extraordinary carrying distance of 4,200 miles, meaning it could, in theory, make the westbound flight to North America without stopping. In practice, headwinds meant that it still needed to make a scheduled stop in Gander. Stratocruisers represented the height of luxury during the 1950s, complete with overhead beds. Passengers on Pam Am Stratocruisers during the period also enjoyed catering by Maxim's of Paris.

- This overhead view of New York City is one of the most detailed in poster history, accurately representing most of Manhattan Island and its surroundings. From the lower left, the New Jersey shoreline is visible, up through the Hudson River toward the George Washington Bridge. The depiction of the East River includes the three lower crossings of the Brooklyn, Manhattan, and Williamsburg Bridges, as well as nearby Roosevelt Island and the Queensboro Bridge. The unknown designer even included the smoke emitted from factories in Greenpoint, Brooklyn, and the north end of Corlears Hook in Manhattan, alluding to the city's industrial history. The Downtown and Midtown skylines, with colorful towers and apartment buildings stretching along Fifth Avenue, are also depicted in rich detail.

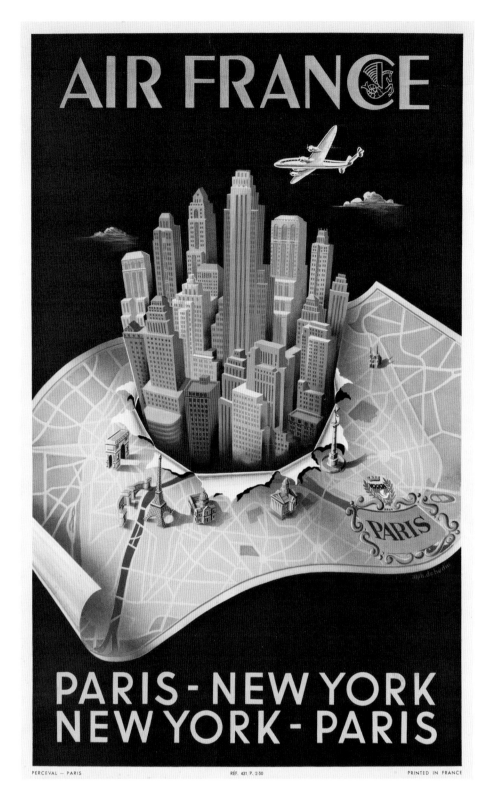

PERCEVAL -- PARIS   RÉF. 431. P. 2.50   PRINTED IN FRANCE

Air France/Paris–New York, 1950

Alphonse Dehédin (Dates Unknown)
*Image Courtesy of Swann
Auction Galleries*

- In an unlikely design for Air France, New York, the insurgent contender for the position of "Greatest City in the World," is seen bursting through a map of Paris, one of the older heavyweight champions for the title.

- The muted colors of Paris contrast with the vibrant multicolored hues of the New York skyscrapers, reinforcing the drama and visual appeal of the modern city.

- While more visually impactful, the skyscrapers look almost as if they are made of children's building blocks and do not represent any obvious structures in New York City. By contrast, the Parisian landmarks, including the Eiffel Tower and the Arc de Triomphe, are clearly discernible.

AIR FRANCE

AMERIQUE DU NORD

EVEN

ABOVE

Air France/Amérique du Nord, 1950

Jean Even (1910–86)
Poster Photo Archives, Posters Please, Inc., NYC

- In addition to his work for Air France, Jean Even produced posters for Evian, the Moroccan tourism board, and Crédit Agricole. He was also the official artist for the French navy during the 1950s.

- Although this design promotes travel to North America in general, only New York is shown (as in the poster by Bayle, see page 134). Here, however, Paris is relegated to the background.

- The image focuses on Midtown Manhattan from Forty-Second Street looking north; the Chrysler Building is thus represented as the tallest in the city, nearly piercing the F in Air France. To the right is the Chanin Building, while the New York Central Building is shown on the far left. A Lockheed Constellation flies above the scene.

OPPOSITE

Swissair/United States, c. 1951

Henri Ott (1919–2009)
Image Courtesy of Swann Auction Galleries

- This photomontage design by Henri Ott proudly announces that Swissair uses Douglas DC-6B aircraft for flights to the United States. Assisted by tailwinds, these planes could fly nonstop on the eastbound journey to Europe, however, they always had to make stops at Gander, Newfoundland, and occasionally, also in Shannon, Ireland, on westbound flights.

- Variants of this poster note that passengers could connect to other US destinations through a partnership with United Air Lines, a feature that continues today through code-share programs. The building here is the RCA Tower at Rockefeller Center; the Swiss National Travel Office would have had a clear view of this structure when it moved to 10 West Forty-Ninth Street in 1951.

- European airfare pricing was based on the British pound until 1949, at which point a devaluation of that currency caused chaos in the industry. Swissair had to be rescued from bankruptcy, and the Swiss government—which owned 30 percent of the airline—bought two new DC-6B planes and leased them to the company. In 1955, the airline was finally profitable enough to buy the planes outright.

SWISSAIR

By Swissair to the United States

DOUGLAS DC-6B

Air France/Paris–New York, 1951

Vincent Guerra (Dates Unknown)
Image Courtesy of Swann Auction Galleries

- This Air France poster again combines French and North American imagery, juxtaposing a relaxed scene along the Champs-Élysées with a star-spangled night sky that illuminates the Statue of Liberty. At the upper left, the famed Lockheed Constellation flies toward New York.

- Nestled within the C of France is a winged seahorse composed of the bust of Pegasus from Greek mythology and the tail of the Dragon of Annam, a Vietnamese symbol. This creature was the original emblem of Air Orient, one of the founding airlines of Air France, and was incorporated into the brand's logo when it was created. The motif was updated by Charles Loupot in 1951, the year this poster was printed.

- This winged seahorse was a holdover from the era when seaplanes played a key role in long-distance air travel, symbolically marrying the sea and the air. It became affectionately known as "the shrimp" by Air France employees.

Frankfurt–USA/Swissair, 1951

Henri Ott (1919–2009)
*Collection Galerie 1 2 3 - Geneva/
Switzerland
www.galerie123.com*

- West Germany did not have an airline
  that flew transatlantic routes until 1955.
  Swissair took advantage of this, offering
  service to a variety of West German
  destinations from the United States.

- Swiss neutrality during World War
  II allowed Swissair to easily obtain
  foreign landing rights in the aftermath,

quickly offering international service to
destinations other airlines could not. In
addition to its unique ports of call, the
stereotypically Swiss virtues of punctu-
ality and cleanliness were deployed in
its advertising.

- In 1951, Henri Ott was commissioned to
  produce a series of posters for Swissair
  as it rolled out the DC-6B aircraft for its
  long-haul routes. He designed a variety
  of linocut images in vibrant colors, with
  this one for the United States focusing
  on the skyscrapers of New York City.

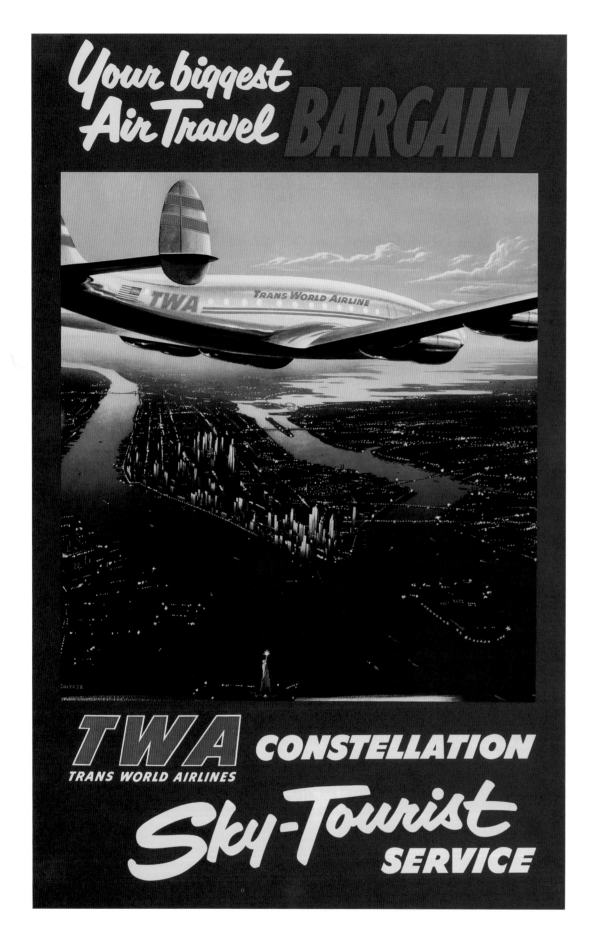

TWA/Sky-Tourist Service,
c. 1952

Frank Soltesz (1912–86)
*Image Courtesy of Swann
Auction Galleries*

- In 1951, TWA's main competitor, Pan Am, flew the DC-6B "Super Six" with the newly invented tourist class. TWA responded by changing the seat layout of some of its existing Constellations to incorporate lower-priced seats. Prior to this, airlines had largely focused on high-end transatlantic passengers.

- In 1946, the International Air Transport Association (IATA) was established and given immunity from US antitrust law. At that time, it set the price for all round-trip transatlantic travel at $711. In 1952, the median annual US income was $2,300—up from $1,400 just six years earlier—making international air travel an incredible expense for the average person. When the new round-trip fare in tourist class was introduced in 1952, the IATA set the cost at $486, making air travel slightly more accessible.

- While this poster promotes the "bargain" service aboard TWA's Constellation aircraft, it still had considerable mystique; the same type of plane was regularly used by President Eisenhower for official government business.

To New York/KLM, 1953

Joop Geesink (1913–84)
*Image Courtesy of Swann
Auction Galleries*

- Founded in 1919, KLM is the oldest airline in the world still in operation. It was also the first continental European airline to fly a scheduled service to New York, starting in May 1946.

- Although KLM's first flight to New York City was with a Douglas DC-4, this poster features the more popular Lockheed Constellation. As the first pressurized airliner in widespread use, this plane could fly above turbulence while consuming less fuel, enabling both more comfortable and longer-haul flights.

- KLM printed this poster by the prolific Dutch designer and cartoonist Joop Geesink with alternate text indicating that the company served fifty-six countries "quickly and comfortably."

B·W·I·A

B·O·A·C

NEW YORK

 BRITISH WEST INDIAN AIRWAYS, AN ASSOCIATE OF BRITISH OVERSEAS AIRWAYS CORPORATION ➤

B.W.I.A./B.O.A.C./New York,
c. 1955

Aldo Cosomati (1895–1977)
*Image Courtesy of Swann
Auction Galleries*

- Aldo Cosomati was one of a number of designers employed by BOAC in the 1950s, creating a handful of posters for a variety of international destinations. Like many commercial illustrators based in Great Britain, he is also known for his work for the London Underground.

- Here, the airline's Vickers Viscount plane is shown flying past the iconic Manhattan skyline.

- In 1949, BWIA became a subsidiary of BOAC, allowing passengers to book connecting flights on either carrier. In this instance, BOAC provided long-haul service over the Atlantic while BWIA handled various Caribbean destinations, most notably Barbados and Trinidad.

Swissair to the USA, 1958

Donald Brun (1909–99)
*Poster House Permanent Collection
Image Courtesy of Poster House*

- From the late nineteenth century, poster designers commonly used formulaic images of Indigenous peoples and local culture to promote certain destinations. Native peoples of the Americas were frequently included in travel posters, "exotifying" the location and imbuing it with an air of "authenticity," no matter how ridiculous the construct.

- This is one of four posters Donald Brun designed in 1958 for Swissair, each of which shows a person in the traditional attire of their homeland. While inappropriate and promoting stereotypes, this design is especially insensitive given that the Lenape people inadvertently "sold" Manhattan to the Dutch in 1626 and were subsequently forced off their ancestral land.

- In contrast to Brun's other posters, this composition combines the historical with the modern—two universally recognized signs of the New World, an Indigenous person and a skyscraper, graphically interwoven with an architectural interpretation of the American flag.

- Europeans, particularly Germans, have a long-standing fascination with Native American culture. Fictional stories of the American frontier were spread through the exceptionally popular writings of the German author Karl May, most notably his 1893 Winnetou trilogy, which influenced European views of Indigenous peoples.

New York/National, 1958

Designer Unknown
Image Courtesy of Illustration Gallery

- National Airlines concentrated on providing service from its base in Florida to the East and Gulf Coasts of the United States. Here, a moody photographic image of the city, with the United Nations Secretariat Building and the Chrysler Building prominently

featured under darkening skies, is used to promote travel to New York.

- Between 1950 and 1959, the carrier used the tagline the "Airline of the Stars" to suggest that Hollywood celebrities used its services, especially between Miami and New York. Although National does not seem to have been given any particular celebrity endorsement, Miami, one of its major destinations, was known as a Hollywood hot spot.

- In December 1958, National became the first airline to fly jets on the Miami to New York route after leasing a Boeing 707 from Pan Am. It proudly advertised the journey as taking two hours and fifteen minutes, as opposed to the three hours and forty minutes it would have taken a DC-7 propeller plane of the period.

New York/Capital Airlines, 1960

Designer Unknown
Image Courtesy of Illustration Gallery

• Between 1958 and 1960, Capital Airlines's planes were involved in a series of fatal accidents. These horrific incidents, as well as the acquisition of several Vickers Viscount planes it could not afford, jeopardized its future. This poster was produced the year before Capital merged with United Air Lines.

• This photographic view over the top of the Brooklyn Bridge captures the illuminated downtown skyline, focusing especially on the buildings at 20 Exchange Place, 70 Pine Street, and 40 Wall Street.

USA/SABENA, c. 1960

Designer Unknown
Image Courtesy of The Ross Art Group Inc.

- Created around the same time as a series of posters produced in-house by Gaston van den Eynde for SABENA, this composition incorporates an evening view of the city skyline across the East River to Manhattan that is nearly identical to van den Eynde's one for North America (see page 194). The main difference is that while his design is highly graphic in style, this anonymous image is expressionistic and painterly.

- As in the other poster, the skyline includes the United Nations headquarters and the Empire State and Chrysler Buildings, all illuminated and reflected in the glassy surface of the East River. Above, a Boeing 707 crosses a stormy sky.

- SABENA is an acronym for Société Anonyme Belge d'Exploitation de la Navigation Aérienne (Belgian Corporation for Air Navigation Services). It began offering flights in the 1930s, providing service primarily to European destinations and the Belgian colonies. SABENA was the national airline for Belgium until 2001, when its assets were sold to what would become Brussels Airlines.

New York/Aer Lingus, c. 1960

Adolph Treidler (1886–1981)
The Collection of Berick Treidler & Lian Dolan
Image Courtesy of Poster House

- Aer Lingus officially entered the Jet Age in 1960, when it incorporated Boeing 720s in its overseas routes to Boston and New York. As this poster features a Lockheed Constellation in the upper register, the design had to be printed before that technological development.

- This gritty and majestic image of New York, presenting the active harbor and dynamic skyline of Manhattan as seen across New York Bay from Governors Island, is clearly based on a photograph. Also visible are the Manhattan Company Building, the City Bank–Farmers Trust Company Building, and the Cities Service Building in the Financial District, as well as Whitehall Terminal in the foreground.

- The artist playfully includes a bright yellow "Visit Ireland" billboard along the waterfront for added effect.

ALITALIA AIRLINES

New York/Alitalia, c. 1960

Designer Unknown
Private Collection, New York
Image Courtesy of Poster House

- Here, an anonymous designer employs a clever typographic conceit somewhere between an ambigram and a pictorial alphabet, in which the buildings of Manhattan's skyline and their corresponding reflection in the river spell out the name of the city.

- Alitalia was founded in 1946 under the name Alitalia-Aerolinee Italiane Internazionali. In 1957, it merged with two smaller companies and adopted the name "Alitalia."

- The company entered the Jet Age in 1960, expanding its international destinations that same year, when the Olympic Games were held in Rome. Throughout the 1960s, Alitalia invested heavily in Rome's new Leonardo da Vinci–Fiumicino Airport, its new hub. It ceased operations in 2021, after it was sold to ITA Airways.

New York Airways, c. 1962

Designer Unknown
Image Courtesy of Swann
Auction Galleries

- New York Airways began flying passengers from Manhattan's West Thirtieth Street Heliport to Idlewild Airport (now known as John F. Kennedy Airport) in 1953. In 1962, it introduced the twin-turbine Boeing Vertol 107-II on a route from the Downtown Manhattan Heliport that had opened in late 1960. Flights to JFK took ten minutes.

- In 1957, New York Airways hired Perry H. Young Jr., the first Black American pilot to be hired by an American airline for regularly scheduled service. He flew for New York Airways until 1979, when the airline filed for bankruptcy. Young had previously made history as the first Black American flight instructor for the United States Army Air Corps.

- Between 1965 and 1967, New York Airways also flew from the top of the Pan Am Building (now the MetLife Building) at Park Avenue and Forty-Fifth Street to JFK Airport; however, this was stopped due to noise complaints. These flights resumed in 1977, but they were shut down again after only three months following an accident in which one of the helicopters toppled on the roof, killing five people.

to get around New York best

...go over it !

NEW YORK AIRWAYS

PRINTED IN SPAIN. REALIZADO EN EL ESTUDIO DE ARTE, DEPARTAMENTO DE PUBLICIDAD DE IBERIA

Lineas Aéreas de España. Depósito Legal M 11987 - 66

Iberia/New York, 1966

Designer Unknown
Private Collection, New York
Image Courtesy of Poster House

- In this clever design, the name of the city, composed of skyscrapers, forms a stylized version of New York's celebrated skyline. The designer plays with the height of the letters, even turning one into the Empire State Building, complete with spire. In the foreground, tugboats and trawlers populate the river, a reference to the city's busy harbor and great nautical heritage.

- A similar typomorphic construction, in which letters are turned into a cityscape, was used for the title treatment in the poster for Woody Allen's 1979 film *Manhattan*. Here, however, is the first time this kind of typographic motif appears in a poster.

- Iberia began direct service to New York in 1954 aboard its Lockheed Super Constellation. The airline acquired and began operating three DC-8s in 1961, one of which is shown at the upper right.

USA/SABENA, 1967

Designer Unknown
Private Collection, New York
Image Courtesy of Poster House

- This poster depicts a view of Manhattan's skyline as if seen through a rain-streaked window, with rays of light extending from the river to the sky as they are reflected in the water. The fact that the city's skyline can be so abstracted and yet still recognizable underscores its iconic status.

- Unlike the rest of the composition, the airplane is clearly depicted. In 1960, the Belgian airline SABENA began using Boeing 707s, one of which is used here, for its transatlantic routes. Here, the company's prominent S is visible on the tail fin.

By the time David Klein designed his now-iconic TWA New York travel poster in 1956 showing the Lockheed Constellation, his advertising work for Broadway had been drawing New Yorkers into theaters for nearly a decade, almost as long as the airline had been enticing travelers to fly Trans World Airlines to cities around the United States and across Europe. As an art director for the advertising agency Clifford Strohl Associates since 1947, Klein had demonstrated an eye for the spectacle of the city, and his playful, energetic style beguiled tourists from near and far.

During the 1940s, when Klein was hitting his stride as a designer, TWA had, in turn, been establishing itself as the most glamorous of the air services, and its role in transporting Hollywood notables from Los Angeles to Paris, Cairo, and New York earned it the designation "airline to the stars." While considerable credit for this can be given to Howard Hughes, who owned a controlling interest in TWA from 1939 until the late 1960s—much is also due to Klein, whose lively illustrations and layered compositions captivated international travelers with promises of "Culture! History! Entertainments!" to be found in the airline's ever-expanding map of prime destinations.

Air travel retained its allure as an ultramodern luxury throughout much of the twentieth century, one that did not become broadly democratized—"air travel for all"—until at least the 1970s. New York journalist Igor Cassini first coined the term that became synonymous with the high-society types who traveled the world in order to attend exclusive parties, premieres, and galas: the jet set. The transoceanic traveler aboard the luxury liners of the 1920s and '30s became the upper-class tourist of the Jet Age during the '50s and '60s, one who could hop on a TWA or Pan Am flight and soar off to destinations across the Americas and Europe.

The elite passengers of the period were well catered to by airlines like TWA, which advertised the cultural sights and events as well as leisure activities on offer in the destination cities. For such tourists, as well as for those who could (and surely did) dream, travel posters did on paper what *Traveltalks*—those short dispatches from Rome or South Africa so sublimely narrated by James FitzPatrick between 1930 and the mid-1950s—did at the movies. They provided glimpses of the wonders travelers might expect to discover at the end of an international flight—visual guides of sorts to the most fascinating locations.

TWA was itself a product of 1960s optimism, as its stylish new terminal—Trans World Flight Center—opened in 1962 at what was then known as Idlewild Airport, renamed John F. Kennedy International Airport in 1963 shortly after the president's assassination. Trans World was intended to serve as a beacon for the splendor of travel from New York City to the rest of the world. And the travelers did come. By 1967, JFK airport was running over 400,000 flights through the New York City metropolitan area, and the city's tourism steadily rose throughout the 1950s and '60s from both domestic and international travelers.

So what could New York City offer them? Just about everything, as Klein's posters eloquently suggest. His advertisements are almost personal love letters to the city. In his hands, New York is synthesized to its essence. Color, light, and energy; culture, history, and delight. Klein's TWA posters layer icon over icon. They can be seen as palimpsests of the culture-making, history-creating, and future-building metropolis.

Klein's most esoteric poster for TWA, from around 1965 (see page 58), is a paean to an earlier age of New York tourism. Titled with the gothic logotype of the *New York Times* as if to say, "Breaking News! Visit the Seven Wonders of the City!" it provides a walk through parts of New York's history. The Statue of Liberty (dedicated in 1886, its gilded bronze showing hints of the oxidized green cast it took on over time) looms sphinxlike over the Brooklyn Bridge (opened in 1883), which seems to support the bronze statue of Prometheus (installed at Rockefeller Center in 1934). The lady gazes over the relatively diminutive statue of Christopher Columbus (erected at Fifty-Ninth Street and Columbus Avenue at the entrance to Central Park in 1892) to her left.

Meanwhile, St. Patrick's Cathedral (completed in 1879) appears entirely veiled in the ethereal purples and blues of its stained-glass windows, and the Staten Island Ferry (operating since 1817) chugs along in the harbor just below it. The Empire State Building (1931) can be seen in the distance through one of the arches of the Brooklyn Bridge. Finally, the statue of George Washington (1883) on Wall Street, commemorating the site where the first president took the oath of office in 1789, stares into the distance as a TWA jet flies overhead.

Here, Klein mingles some of the great histories and mythologies of New York in a single image. The Prometheus statue also featured in four of his other TWA posters (see pages 168, 196, 203, and 204). The inscription on the sculpture—an eighteen-foot object weighing eight tons that was created by Paul Manship—is an ode to the human ingenuity that created it: "Prometheus, teacher in every art, brought the fire that hath proved to mortals a means to mighty ends."

Klein also plays with the "Monument Valley" approach in another New York poster (c. 1960) for the airline. The image is slightly more abstract, with a more modern, sans-serif type; a riot of scrappily applied color planes in gouache; and an Art Deco sculpture of Atlas supporting a giant armillary sphere (created by Lee Lawrie and Rene Paul Chambellan in 1937) added to the lineup. Here, Klein weaves together past, present, and future in an image promoting the futuristic jets that transport passengers to New York, a city full of historic monuments and modern wonders.

In Klein's more exuberant posters from the 1960s, including three unpublished designs, he offers a guide for tourists: In one of them, for example, lettering in a range of typefaces records the names of some of the unique neighborhoods, cultural offerings, and landmarks of the city as they stream from the Statue of Liberty's torch. In a second poster design, Klein intersperses similarly playful motifs suggesting postcards of the city with lettered signs and street names to construct a fun, if geographically random, vertical street map. Here, he captures a city of dichotomies: the bohemian Greenwich Village of poets and painters alongside the capitalist frenzy of Wall Street and the ostentatious wealth of Park Avenue and the Waldorf Astoria.

The absences in Klein's New York travel posters are clear to contemporary viewers. While he does include the Metropolitan Museum of Art (at Fifth Avenue and Eighty-Second Street and serving as the southernmost point of the corridor known as Museum Mile), Lincoln Center (on the West Side of Manhattan), and the Bronx Zoo, Klein represents no other monuments, neighborhoods, or institutions that might coax tourists above Midtown. He produced no poster dedicated to Black or immigrant New York either. Left out were Harlem with its Apollo Theater (relating to the ancient Greek figures of Prometheus and Atlas featured elsewhere in his work); the hustle-bustle of 125th Street (home to some of the most dynamic cultural hot spots of New York's Black community for decades); and images of Chinatown (in Lower Manhattan) and Jackson Heights, Queens, home in the 1950s to significant immigrant communities from China, South Asia, and Central and South America. The typical tourist imagined by TWA and its designers was not, for the most part, encouraged to visit the outer boroughs at all, though a walk across the Brooklyn Bridge or a ride on the Staten Island Ferry was encouraged.

Klein's most abstract compositions seem to speak most effectively to the drama of New York (see page 58). In this design from around 1960, Lady Liberty, now devoid of color, appears as an object of negative space on which slashes of blue and brown define the drapery, while the tablet she holds remains blank, as if to invite viewers to imagine new lines yet to be written. Enveloped by the night sky, she floats against a collage of red, white, and blue fireworks. There is no sign here of the TWA SuperJet that usually crosses his images from this time, either above or below the central motifs (usually it flew from left to right, but occasionally in the other direction).

The most iconic of Klein's TWA posters is among his earliest (see page 166). It distills the essence of Times Square without actually showing us a single recognizable structure. The Great White Way? In Klein's version,

travelers are welcomed to the great multicolor way. It is an avenue of bright hues and hyperkinetic energy, a view of New York as seen from Broadway, through Times Square, and beyond. The SuperJet—always traveling to the next destination—traverses the highest point of the poster's horizon line, a conduit to the real experience: the life of the city. While all of Klein's TWA New York travel posters delight, this one—the most archetypal and the most abstract—stands apart. It perfectly captures the exhilaration of the Jet Age and the postwar optimism of New York City.

Of Klein's many TWA travel and tourism posters, this is the one that has proved so enduringly popular that it appears in every guest room at the TWA Hotel that opened at JFK Airport in 2019. In this composition and its variants, the details are left to the imagination. Its neon glow attracts the eye to the city grid and the city lights. The glittering metropolis is always in motion, beckoning, welcoming, overwhelming. Bubbly lights suggest the flash of paparazzi cameras, glowing streetlights, or just the vibrant energy of city dwellers beneath the jet stream of the TWA flight as it exits the cityscape. Klein's image of New York is one that both tourists and locals might recognize as representing its quintessential character. The defining element here is not to be found in the statues or the street names, but in the pulsing energy of the city itself. Even the boldface logotype of "New York" reflects the lights from below, illuminating the SuperJet above. Nothing can contain the radiance of Times Square, the multilayered symbol of twentieth-century urban entertainment.

The neon lights of the 1950s and '60s lit up Broadway theaters showing plays that reflected a popular fascination with recent and distant histories, including *Camelot*, *A Funny Thing Happened on the Way to the Forum*, *Bye Bye Birdie*, *Funny Girl*, *Carnival!*, *Fiddler on the Roof*, *The Sound of Music*, and *Cabaret*. Meanwhile, new productions used music, lyrics, and drama to hold up a mirror to some of the radical cultural changes occurring across the country. Musical hits like *West Side Story* (which addressed bigotry and racial tensions on the West Side of Manhattan), *Hair* (which offered a vision of a more liberated, youthful, and peaceful future), and *How to Succeed in Business Without Really Trying* (which satirized the American obsession with self-help as the path to the American dream) appealed to a new kind of audience. For the generation that came of age in the early '60s, the optimism of the previous decade was starting to shift. But New York remained a center of progressive cultural discourse.

David Klein's love for the city—in color and composition—is so apparent in the TWA posters that invited travelers to New York to enjoy the energy and delight of a uniquely vibrant urban environment. They are vivid portraits of this city's cultural richness and distinctive character.

In 1962, Eero Saarinen's space-age Trans World Airlines Flight Center had opened at JFK Airport, becoming a landmark destination in itself. By the end of that decade, the airline was carrying more passengers across the world, and between more destinations, than any other. Air travel was becoming more accessible to many, and the tourist industry in New York continued to thrive, flying passengers to visit the sights of New York City from Los Angeles, Mexico City, London, and Bombay (now Mumbai).

While TWA eventually shut down in 2001 following three decades of internal strife as a result of the 1970s oil crisis, mismanagement, and high-profile accidents, air travel to New York remains as popular as ever, thanks in part to the work of David Klein. And Klein's most-iconic poster has retained its resonance for those with dreams of inviting interstellar voyagers to our shores, as the Orbitz travel agency suggested in its 2001 ad series "Visit Planet Earth" (see page 173), featuring Klein's original Times Square illustration.

After David Klein's work with TWA ended, he continued to design travel and tourism posters, including a series of ads for Amtrak that beckoned American travelers back to the railways to see the country by land. But that TWA poster of Times Square—with its Jet Age optimism and glamour—remains iconic.

TIMES SQUARE: THE HEART OF NEW YORK

Times Square is not just Forty-Second Street and Broadway. It is a five-block stretch from Forty-Second Street to Forty-Seventh Street—a bow-tie shaped area formed by the crossing of Broadway and Seventh Avenue at Forty-Fifth Street—from which it gets its nickname, the Crossroads of the World. It was once the center of New York's horse-and-carriage industry and was known as Longacre Square after Long Acre in London, the old home of that city's coach and carriage makers. As Lower Manhattan became increasingly commercial and industrial, theaters and other establishments moved farther uptown, ultimately settling in this district.

Two seminal events in 1904 enhanced the renown of Times Square: the opening of New York's first underground subway line—with a stop at Forty-Second Street and Broadway—and the decision to construct the new headquarters of the *New York Times* at One Times Square, right at Forty-Second Street and Broadway. In April of that year, New York's mayor, then George B. McClellan Jr., officially named the area Times Square in honor of its most illustrious tenant. While the *New York Times* would relocate to Forty-Third Street in 1913, the name was there to stay. In 1907, Times Square was the site of the first New Year's Eve ball drop, an annual event that is still held there today.

OPPOSITE

Fly BCPA to America, c. 1947

Keith Howland (1925–2004)
Private Collection, New York
Image Courtesy of Poster House

- This poster highlights two of Times Square's most legendary advertisements: the neon Wrigley's Spearmint gum sign—in place from 1936 to 1960—that featured

colorful tropical fish blowing bubbles next to a pack of gum, and the electric-light and neon billboard for Camel cigarettes—installed between 1941 and 1946—that featured the Camel Man blowing four-foot-high "smoke" rings from his mouth.

- The Wrigley's sign, originally created by graphic designer Dorothy Shepard, was replaced in 1948 by the equally famous Bond Clothing Stores's waterfall—a

masterpiece by Douglas Leigh, an advertising wunderkind of the era.

- Keith Howland designed several posters for British Commonwealth Pacific Airlines (BCPA) during its seven years of operation between 1947 and 1954 (when it was taken over by Qantas). This composition captures the brief moment between the founding of the airline and the removal of the Wrigley's sign.

- Also visible on the New York Times Building is its famous "zipper"—an electric news ticker composed of almost fifteen thousand light bulbs.

B.O.A.C., 1950

Frank Wootton (1914–98)
Private Collection, New York
Image Courtesy of Poster House

- While this poster promotes travel to the United States, New York City is once again used as emblematic of the country as a whole. Although the poster was printed in numerous languages, this variant was aimed at Spanish-speaking viewers.

- This quintessential view of the city does not focus on recognizable sights such as the lights of Broadway or Times Square, but provides an evocative glimpse of the countless illuminated windows of Midtown office buildings and the glow of streetlights on a rainy night.

- An unmistakably American addition to the urban landscape, the 1949 Chevrolet Deluxe two-door sedan in the foreground was in production between 1941 and 1952. A large vehicle of this kind would

have been especially fascinating to a European viewer of the poster.

- At the upper right, a Boeing 377 Stratocruiser, recognizable by its bulbous nose, speeds through the night sky. The aircraft, which went into service for BOAC in 1950, was based on the design for the B-29 Superfortress used during World War II, and was designed to compete with the Lockheed Constellation and the Douglas DC-6.

Scandinavian Airlines System/ New York, 1952

Otto Nielsen (1916–2000)
Private Collection, New York
Image Courtesy of Poster House

- This poster shows the glamorous hustle and bustle of Times Square and the fashionable crowd in the streets beneath the New York Times Building from which the area derives its name. While not expressly depicted, the pervasive neon glow associated with the area is reflected in the composition's vibrant tones.

- The *New York Times* was a tenant in its namesake building at One Times Square between 1905 and 1913, when it moved to its new headquarters on Forty-Third Street. Shown here is the original *Times* sign near the top of the building, which remained there after the newspaper relocated. Also visible are the letters *enex*, part of the famous neon Kleenex installation featuring the comic-strip character Little Lulu, a feature of Times Square from the late 1940s through the mid-1960s.

- This is one of a few posters that highlight the area's architecture, most notably through the inclusion in the background of the Continental Building, completed in 1931 at Forty-First Street and Broadway.

- Scandinavian Airlines Systems (SAS) was founded in 1946 through the conglomeration of three existing airlines from Denmark, Sweden, and Norway. That same year, the company inaugurated its first flight from Stockholm to New York.

fly by **B·O·A·C**

u·s·a

HOTEL

BRITISH OVERSEAS AIRWAYS CORPORATION IN ASSOCIATION WITH QANTAS EMPIRE AIRWAYS LIMITED · SOUTH AFRICAN AIRWAYS · TASMAN EMPIRE AIRWAYS LIMITED

OPPOSITE

B.O.A.C./U.S.A., 1954

Dick Negus (1927–2011) &
Philip Sharland (1923–86)
Private Collection, New York
Image Courtesy of Poster House

- In what might be seen as a precursor to David Klein's poster for TWA showing Times Square (see page 166), this composition, filled with abstract representations of buildings, lights, neon signs, and rapidly flowing traffic, is the first to apply rudimentary Atomic Era design principles to an advertisement for travel to America. Although it does not mention New York by name, the visual connection to Times Square is obvious.

- Unlike Klein's TWA poster, however, this image bears no resemblance to the actual Times Square. Instead, Negus and Sharland present an imaginary cityscape that suggests the vibrant, pulsating energy at the heart of New York.

RIGHT

New York/Capital Airlines,
c. 1955

Designer Unknown
Image Courtesy of Swann
Auction Galleries

- Here, a stream of brightly lit theater awnings and stores suggests Times Square at night as a fiery canyon opening between the skyscrapers. At left is the New York Times Building, and next to it the Paramount Building, home then to the Paramount Theater that featured film screenings as well as the top performers of the era, among them Frank Sinatra, Ella Fitzgerald, Louis Armstrong, Henny Youngman, Dean Martin, and Jerry Lewis. Like the Scandinavian Airlines poster (see page 163), this one also shows one of the neon Kleenex signs that remained a familiar feature of Times Square between the late 1940s and the mid-1960s.

- In spite of all the showbiz glitz, however, the somewhat hellish nature of this image was not entirely inappropriate. During the Great Depression, the area became increasingly seedy, and during World War II, servicemen on leave came to Times Square seeking erotic entertainment as well as cheap hotels and restaurants. By the 1950s, various unsavory businesses were proliferating there virtually unchecked.

- During this decade, Capital Airlines, headquartered at the new Washington National Airport in Arlington, Virginia, was the fifth-largest domestic carrier in the United States. In 1948, Capital had already distinguished itself by introducing one of the first economy-class services, the "Nighthawk" between Chicago and New York. It also installed the first airborne televisions on some of its other flights. The main aim was to compete with the railroads for passengers who could not usually afford to travel by air.

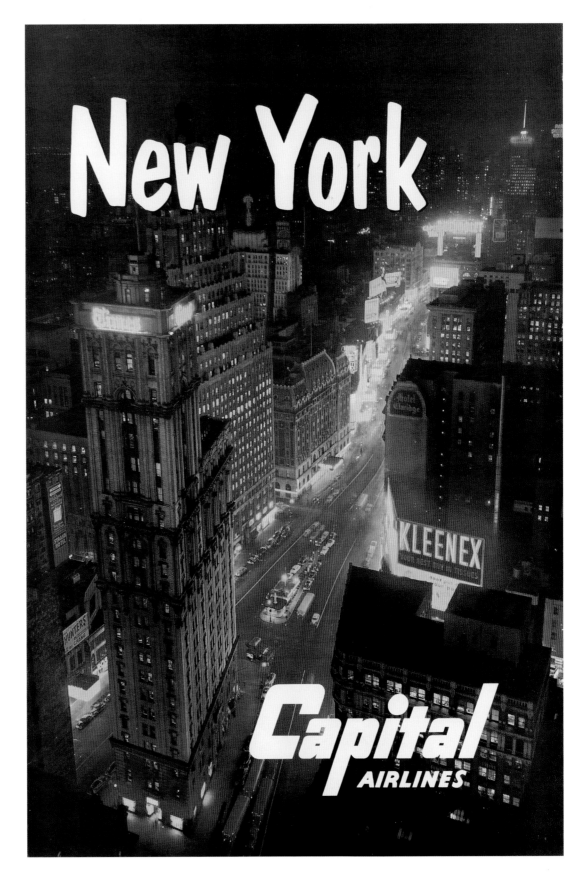

NEW YORK

FLY THERE BY **QANTAS**

AUSTRALIA'S ROUND-THE-WORLD AIRLINE

New York/TWA, 1956

David Klein (1918–2005)
Private Collection, New York
Image Courtesy of Poster House

- One of the most famous graphic images of New York, this poster depicts a kaleidoscopic, abstract view of Times Square looking north toward Forty-Seventh Street. With his brilliant use of colorful geometry, Klein deftly evokes the billboards, lights, traffic, energy, and excitement of the area.

- The composition contains two discernible pictographic landmarks within Times Square that serve to orientate the viewer's perspective. At the top of the central building is the yellow Chevrolet logo—a neon sign that was in place from

the 1920s through the early 1960s. On the lower section of that same building is also the recognizable swoosh of the Pepsi logo installed there between the mid-1940s and the middle of the following decade.

- This poster proved so popular that it was reprinted multiple times. This, however, is the rare first edition of the design that features a detailed image of a TWA Lockheed Constellation above the text. As TWA entered the Jet Age, later versions replaced this propeller aircraft with a simple silhouette of a jet plane.

- A year after it was issued, a copy of this poster was acquired by the Museum of Modern Art for its permanent collection and was included in the institution's earliest travel-poster exhibition in the spring of 1957.

New York/Qantas, c. 1958

Harry Rogers (1929–2012)
Private Collection, New York
Image Courtesy of Poster House

- This poster depicts a charming twilight scene in Times Square, looking north. The giant Pepsi sign on the right was in place from 1955 to 1960, replacing the famous Bond waterfall.

- The statue of the composer George M. Cohan on the corner of Forty-Sixth Street and Broadway is notably absent from the image as it was not installed until 1959—these types of visual clues help poster historians ascribe a time period to an undated work.

- The city's multicolored taxicabs are another interesting detail—they did not adopt their uniform yellow color until 1967.

- Qantas began its "round the world service" in 1958, with Super Constellations leaving from Melbourne flying both to the East and to the West. It was the only international airline at the time that had the right to operate across the United States.

LEFT

New York/Fly TWA Jets, c. 1960

David Klein (1918–2005)
Private Collection, New York
Image Courtesy of Poster House

- This painted study for an unrealized poster presents Paul Manship's recumbent Prometheus sculpture removed from Rockefeller Center and set against a dazzling evening cityscape.

- While none of the buildings are recognizable, one can still discern billboards, neon signs, and advertising signs.

- As in Klein's poster for TWA featuring Times Square (see page 166), each structure is irregular in form and unique in color, size, and shape.

OPPOSITE

New York/Northeast, c. 1961

Charles Robert Perrin (1915–99)
Private Collection, New York
Image Courtesy of Poster House

- Rather than focus on notable landmarks or famous buildings, Charles Perrin highlights two of the city's equally pervasive but less glamorous features: pigeons and a hot dog cart.

- While his focus is on the sheer variety of people crowding the city's streets, Perrin also documents the signs of many of Times Square's most notable advertisers in the background: Anheuser-Busch, Chevrolet, Canadian Club, Admiral, and Howard Johnson.

- He also includes electrified, cast-iron, twin-lamp posts, which first appeared in New York in 1892, when fifty of them were installed on Fifth Avenue.

- Northeast Airlines was formed in 1940, ultimately merging with Delta Air Lines in 1972. It began using Convair 880 jets in 1960, indicating that this poster, which features one in the upper register, could not have been printed before that date. By 1966, Northeast Airlines had changed its livery to yellow and white, and its planes became known as the Yellowbirds.

NEW YORK

NORTHEAST
AIRLINES

USA/Aer Lingus, c. 1962

Designer Unknown
Image Courtesy of Affiche Passion

- Times Square represented an unlikely promotional lure for Aer Lingus during the early 1960s. At this point, even the *New York Times*, after whose building the area had originally been named, was forced to describe Forty-Second Street as "the worst block in town."

- In 1960, the airline entered the Jet Age, acquiring three speedy Boeing 720s for its transatlantic service, and in 1964 it built on this success by investing in the larger Boeing 707s for its New York passengers. Aer Lingus was flying more passengers than ever to New York.

- But Times Square remained a tourist destination, if an unsavory one. If any of these unsuspecting travelers, inspired by the poster, had actually chosen to explore the area during their visit, perhaps en route to see a popular Broadway show like *My Fair Lady*, more than a few might have been shocked by the seediness of an area then dominated by sex shops, drug deals, prostitution, and gang violence. Times Square had, in fact, become a prime symbol of the decline of the great city.

New York/American Airlines, c. 1965

Frederick E. Conway (1900–73)
Private Collection, New York
Image Courtesy of Poster House

- This poster shows an imaginary, rainy view of Times Square at night. The lights, as if seen through a streaked car window, blur above the slick streets as the colors merge into pinwheels and splotches.

- Perhaps suggesting the experience of a tourist overwhelmed by the sights and sounds of the area, the image exposes the viewer to a jumble of signage that represents the essence of Times Square but not its reality. Although designed to look like an actual snapshot of the theater district, many of the signs in this poster did not actually exist or were situated elsewhere in the neighborhood.

- Two pop-culture references help to determine the date of this poster: *Hello Dolly* premiered on Broadway in 1964, and the headline "Gemini Pilots in Orbit" that appears on the news "zipper" would have been announced between 1965 and 1966.

LEFT

New York/Pan Am, c. 1967

Designer Unknown
Private Collection, New York
Image Courtesy of Poster House

- This poster is a collage of snapshots of New York City and its inhabitants toward the end of the 1960s. With images that might have been cut directly from lifestyle magazines of the era, the decoupage composition reflects the vigorous, youthful, sexy side of the metropolis.

- Although a small handful of famous vistas and tourist attractions are included, this advertisement is clearly directed at visitors who do not care about the city's history or its artistic heritage. It is an unabashed celebration of youth culture and New York nightlife.

- The approximate date of this unsigned poster can be determined by the various theatrical performances referenced in the collage. Between 1966 and 1969, Angela Lansbury appeared in the Broadway production of *Mame* at the Winter Garden Theatre. Meanwhile, *You Know I Can't Hear You When the Water's Running* premiered at the Ambassador Theatre in 1967, the same year that *Cactus Flower* with Lauren Bacall opened at the Royale Theatre (now the Bernard B. Jacobs Theatre) and *Cabaret* debuted at the Imperial Theatre.

OPPOSITE

Visit Planet Earth via Orbitz, 2001

David Klein (1918–2005) &
Robert C. Swanson (1920–2016)
Image Courtesy of Affiche Passion

- In 2001, Orbitz, the online travel agency and flight search engine, hired David Klein and Robert C. Swanson to create five images for its first promotional campaign. The idea was to appeal to nostalgia for the early days of popular air travel in the 1950s and '60s, and the kind of "Mad Men" advertising used to sell it. The slogan also suggests an invitation to imagined extraterrestrials considering a trip.

- This image is adapted from a poster design Klein made for TWA in 1956 (see page 166). Planet Earth is symbolized here not by nature or even by natural forms as one might expect, but by the bright lights and electronic billboards of Times Square, effects made possible by modern technology. The tiny yellow cab in the foreground appears to be driving along the avenue into a brilliant, high-tech future.

- As many of the posters here demonstrate, Klein had been a key figure in travel design during the '50s and '60s. And while Swanson was probably best known as the "King of Jingles" between 1952 and 1978, writing ditties for such products as Campbell's soups, Schaefer beer, and Winston cigarettes, he also produced graphic designs for TWA during the 1950s. Both men were in their eighties when they undertook this project for Orbitz.

VISIT PLANET EARTH VIA ORBITZ

The World's Leading Airlines bring you the most low fares at ORBITZ.COM

STREEETSCAPES & URBAN OASES

In addition to its tall buildings, the sheer scale of the chaos and drama of life in New York City seemed to enthrall many who had never experienced it in person. Artists, seeking to convey the symphony of the city's sounds in images, incorporated synesthetic elements in their work. Much like cinematographers, poster designers had to set the scene for people not familiar with the city. For some of them, New York meant the "concrete" or "asphalt" jungle—two terms that first emerged in the 1920s. For others, it was a visual "city symphony," a representation of the disorder and confusion of modern life, while a few chose to focus on the quieter, more peaceful, and even romantic parts of the city tucked away between the tall buildings, offering respite from the frenetic pace.

OPPOSITE

New York/United Air Lines, c. 1950

Joseph Feher (1908–87)
Poster House Permanent Collection
Image Courtesy of Poster House

- Rather than focusing exclusively on the impressive cityscape, Joseph Feher juxtaposes the urban with the pastoral. The foreground is dominated by a picturesque rendering of the Gapstow Bridge over the Pond in Central Park. Behind it stand several Fifth Avenue landmarks, including the Sherry-Netherland Hotel, the Savoy-Plaza Hotel (replaced by the General Motors Building in 1968), and the Squibb Building, as well as a sliver of the celebrated Plaza Hotel.

- The plane at the upper right is a Douglas DC-6 that United Airlines brought into service in the late 1940s. Known as the Skymaster, it was an updated version of the DC-4 and was the main competitor to the Lockheed Constellation used by other airlines.

NEW YORK

Fly NORTHWEST Orient AIRLINES

New York/Northwest Orient Airlines, c. 1950

Designer Unknown
Poster Photo Archives, Posters Please, Inc., NYC

- In 1949, Northwest Orient Airlines and three other carriers began flying Boeing Stratocruisers, one of which is shown here above a collaged view of Manhattan highlighting the Statue of Liberty, the Staten Island Ferry, the Brooklyn Bridge, and many of the city's most notable buildings.

- Northwest received controversial funding and support from the US government for its Stratocruisers, including a generous contract to carry mail along its routes to Hawaii and the western Pacific Islands. Only fifty-five production versions of the plane were ever built, and, in 1960, Northwest was the last airline to phase them out.

- Although the designer of this poster is unknown, all of Northwest's graphic advertising of the period features similar flat planes of color and a pastiche of important local landmarks, suggesting that they are all the work of a single artist.

New York by Clipper, c. 1950

Designer Unknown
Poster Photo Archives, Posters Please, Inc., NYC

- In June 1939, Pan American World Airways introduced its transatlantic Clippers on its new route from Port Washington, New York, to Marseilles, France. Also known as "flying boats," these seaplanes took their name from the great nineteenth-century sailing ships.

- Although, technically, the first scheduled transatlantic flights had been made by German zeppelins in the 1920s, the Clipper was the first fixed-wing passenger aircraft to offer that service. After World War II, Pan Am kept the Clipper name as a marketing tool even when it no longer used seaplanes, as seen in this poster featuring the new Boeing Stratocruiser.

- The phrase "Fly the Leader" on the pennant at the lower left refers to the fact that, until the mid-1940s, Pan Am had a virtual monopoly among US airlines on international flights.

- The montage of New York City highlights here includes the seals of the Central Park Zoo, the Rockettes, a horse-drawn carriage ride through Central Park, Trinity Church on Wall Street, alfresco dining, a night at the ballet, and two anonymous skyscrapers—all crowned by the words *New York* in the light-bulb marquee lettering associated with Broadway shows.

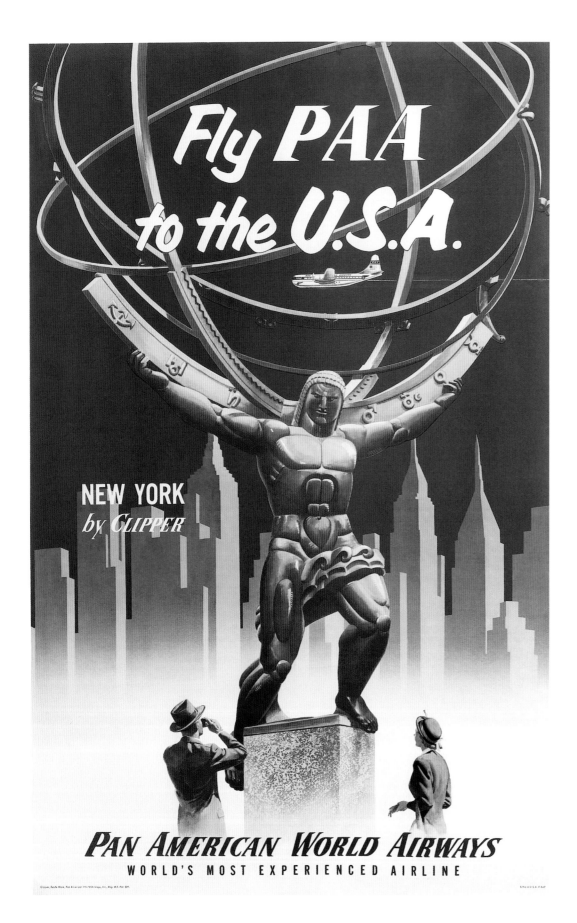

**Fly PAA to the U.S.A./
New York**, c. 1950

Designer Unknown
*Image Courtesy of Swann
Auction Galleries*

- From 1929, Pan American Airways's official emblem (not shown on this poster) was its initials (PAA) inside a globe decorated with longitudinal lines. This symbol is brought to the fore in

this poster dominated by the famous Art Deco statue of Atlas located in Rockefeller Center on Fifth Avenue. Meanwhile, stylized versions of classic Manhattan skyscrapers can be seen in the background.

- The Boeing Stratocruiser, used by Pan American at the time for its long-haul flights across the Pacific and the Atlantic, is shown flying above Atlas's head.

- In 1950, Pan American Airways became Pan American World Airways. Around that time, it also began incorporating the slogan "World's Most Experienced Airline" into many of its advertisements. It was not until 1956 that the airline started using "Pan Am" as shorthand for its brand rather than PAA.

Fly BCPA to America, 1952

Keith Howland (1925–2004)
*Vintage Travel and Advertising Archive /
Alamy Stock Photo*

- Founded in 1946, British Commonwealth
  Pacific Airlines (BCPA) was a joint
  venture among the governments of
  Australia, New Zealand, and the United
  Kingdom, designed to create a network
  of transpacific flights.

- At the time, long-haul flights were
  incredibly complicated and involved
  multiple stops. In 1952, the fastest route

from Sydney, Australia, to New York
would have been: Sydney–Auckland–
Fiji–Canton Island–Hawaii–San
Francisco–Chicago–New York, a journey
of four to five days.

- The street scene in this poster is set at
  the junction of Forty-Second Street and
  Fifth Avenue. While the New York Public
  Library and the Art Deco facade of
  500 Fifth Avenue are visible on the left,
  the composition is slightly imaginary as
  traffic flows south down that avenue,
  putting both buildings on the opposite
  side of the street.

- Keith Howland was an illustrator for
  the Australian advertising agency USP
  Benson. Given the incredible distance,
  time, and cost involved—and considering the geographic inaccuracies in
  the design—it is possible that he did
  not actually visit New York while he was
  working on this poster. In 1954, after
  taking over BCPA's route, the airline
  Qantas used the same design, changing
  only the color of the car in the foreground to blue.

Fly by B.O.A.C./U.S.A., 1952

Fly by B.O.A.C./U.S.A., 1952

Xenia (Dates Unknown)
Private Collection, New York
Image Courtesy of Poster House

- Reminiscent of a postage stamp, this poster shows off a bucolic view of buildings on Fifth Avenue as couples stroll around the Pond in Central Park. Although it is not an entirely accurate depiction, it creates the sense of an oasis within the city.

- When Frederick Law Olmsted and Calvert Vaux designed Central Park, they incorporated existing swampland to create the

Pond. Set below street level, it is a place where visitors can peacefully commune with nature away from the discordant bustle of the city around them.

- BOAC (British Overseas Airways Corporation) was formed in 1939, and began regularly scheduled flights to New York in 1946, aboard either Lockheed Constellations or, starting in 1949, Boeing 377 Stratocruisers—one of which is depicted here. At that time, the journey took almost twenty hours and required stops for refueling in both Shannon, Ireland, and Gander, Newfoundland.

KLM/New York, c. 1952

J.U. Vilendsen (Dates Unknown)
Collection Galerie 1 2 3 - Geneva/
Switzerland
www.galerie123.com

- Starting in the early 1950s, KLM began offering its first-class passengers Delft Blue miniature houses filled with Dutch gin. These souvenirs have become collectors' items and the tradition continues to this day.

- Here, instead of Delftware Dutch buildings, the flight attendant holds a tray of New York skyscrapers—potentially a lot of gin!

- The cityscape on the tray gives a generalized view of Manhattan as seen from the Staten Island Ferry.

New York par

KLM

LIGNES AÉRIENNES ROYALES NÉERLANDAISES

New York/Pennsylvania Railroad, c. 1952

Designer Unknown
Poster Photo Archives, Posters Please, Inc., NYC

- The completion of the United Nations complex in 1952 enabled advertisers to promote an exciting new landmark in the New York landscape. The Pennsylvania Railroad, like many of the national railway lines, included the structure in its advertising to reflect the modernity and soaring optimism of the years after World War II.

- The UN buildings were constructed on land donated by Nelson Rockefeller in 1946. The long, thin seventeen-acre plot along the East River required the ten members of the international design team, overseen by Director of Planning Wallace Harrison, to make certain compromises. In the end, an agreement was reached on designs by Le Corbusier of France and Oscar Niemeyer of Brazil that fit the requisite buildings within the site. This view from north to south shows the General Assembly Building in the foreground, with the Secretariat Building behind it.

- While the buildings are physically located in Manhattan, the area is officially international territory under the sole jurisdiction of the United Nations.

New York/American Airlines, c. 1952

Parker (Dates Unknown)
Image Courtesy of Swann Auction Galleries

- This poster shows the United Nations Secretariat and Assembly Buildings, seen from the East River facing uptown from an unusually low angle. The Chrysler Building is visible on the left, with the tower of the RCA Building at Rockefeller Center standing tallest on the right.

- The same image was used on the cover of the October 1950 issue of *Collier's* magazine. As construction on the UN buildings began in October 1949 and was not completed until 1952, it is likely that this design is based, at least in part, on a rendering rather than a photograph.

Swissair/USA, 1955

Donald Brun (1909–99)
© David Pollack Vintage Posters

- In 1952, Swissair held a competition for the design of its new logo, the results of which are shown in the lower section of this poster. The winning designer, Rudolf Bircher, claimed that the shape of an arrow embodied the essence of flying—getting to a destination quickly and in a straight line.

- This new logo represented both the earliest adoption of modern corporate design principles in the airline industry and was the only airline logo that did not require modification at the advent of the Jet Age in the late 1950s. In fact, it survived until 1981.

- The illustrated perspective in this poster appears to be from within Bryant Park on West Forty-Second Street, looking toward the Chrysler Building on the left.

RIGHT

American Airlines/New York, 1956

Weimer Pursell (1906–74)
Poster House Permanent Collection
Image Courtesy of Poster House

- This dynamic image, with its abstract skyscrapers, shop windows, and traffic-filled streets, is an exceptional example of American mid-century modernism in graphic design. Since it incorporates many of the same conceits as David Klein's TWA poster of Times Square made that same year, it is interesting to consider which came first.

- The large, glass-faced building on the right side of the poster represents a brand-new kind of skyscraper, like the Lever House in Midtown, the first commercial structure in New York City (built between 1950 and 1952) with glass-curtain walls.

UNITED AIR LINES

NEW YORK

United Air Lines/New York, 1957

Joseph Binder (1898–1972)
Poster Houser Permanent Collection
Image Courtesy of Poster House

- This poster is part of a larger series created by Joseph Binder for United Air Lines. In it, he uses the relatively new United Nations Secretariat Building and the curved roof of the General Assembly Building to promote travel to New York.

- Completed in 1951, the Secretariat Building was an architectural triumph and the city's first glass-curtain skyscraper. It was designed in the International Style by a multinational team of ten architects, including Le Corbusier, under the direction of Wallace Harrison (who was also involved in the construction of Rockefeller Center). As the United Nations was meant to function as a symbol of a peaceful, progressive future, its style eschews historical reference in favor of pure modernism.

- The flags arranged outside the United Nations represent its member states, always displayed in alphabetical order. In 1957, there were 82 members; today, there are 193 member states representing every officially recognized country in the world, as well as two observer states, representing the Holy See (Vatican City) and the State of Palestine. In this composition, the flags of Argentina, Australia, Belgium, Bolivia, Brazil, Burma, Byelorussia, Canada, Chile, the Republic of China, Colombia, Costa Rica, Czechoslovakia, Denmark, and the Dominican Republic are visible.

U.S.A./B.O.A.C., 1957

Designer Unknown
Private Collection, New York
Image Courtesy of Poster House

- This is one of British Overseas Airways Corporation's last posters promoting transatlantic travel prior to its entry into the Jet Age. On October 4, 1958, the airline made the first regularly scheduled, commercial jet flight across the Atlantic, flying a redesigned de Havilland Comet 4 and beating its main rival, Pan Am, by three weeks.

- The frenetic street scene, in which cars appear to be going in every direction, perfectly captures the chaotic traffic of Manhattan as experienced by someone unfamiliar with it. Similarly disarranged, the buildings are depicted in an asymmetric, almost naive, expressionist style with uneven and unaligned windows.

- The composition incorporates both imagined and nostalgic motifs: the twin-style bishop's crook lamppost was never installed in Manhattan, and the classic New York bus-stop sign, silhouetted in the foreground, was in use only from the 1920s to the early 1950s.

- As this poster was printed in Great Britain, and published in several different languages, it is conceivable that the artist would not have been aware of these inaccuracies. However, the bus-stop sign still directs attention to the name of the airline, visually emphasizing the brand within the composition.

USA

Flugreisen mit

BOAC

BRITISH OVERSEAS AIRWAYS CORPORATION

UNITED AIR LINES
NEW YORK

NEW YORK

NORTHWEST *Orient* AIRLINES

PRINTED IN U.S.A.

United Air Lines/New York,
c. 1957

Stanley Walter Galli (1912–2009)
Private Collection, New York
Image Courtesy of Poster House

- In this beautiful composition, Stanley Galli shows an elegant couple in a hansom cab as it enters Central Park at Fifty-Ninth Street and Fifth Avenue, representing a quieter, more intimate aspect of New York City life.

- The twilit cityscape behind the romantic tableau includes the William Tecumseh Sherman monument in Grand Army Plaza and the silhouette of the Crown Building on Fifty-Seventh Street and Fifth Avenue.

- While automobiles began outnumbering horses in Manhattan as early as 1912, it was not until 1917 that horse-drawn street cars fell out of use. Horse-drawn carriages were ultimately relegated to Central Park, where they became a permanent part of the city's tourist culture. This practice has become increasingly controversial as animal rights activists protest the use (and abuse) of horses in the carriage industry.

ABOVE

New York/Northwest Orient Airlines, 1958

Designer Unknown
© David Pollack Vintage Posters

- This poster presents a photographic nighttime view looking across Manhattan toward the Chrysler Building. The back of the giant neon sign for Tudor City is visible at the lower left, although its lighting had long ceased to function by the time this poster was produced.

- The image is from an unusual east–west viewpoint, taken at a height that suggests it may have been shot from a helicopter. Photography like this was not common during the 1950s and would not become mainstream within posters until the early 1970s.

U.S.A.

ALITALIA

ARTI GRAFICHE PANETTO & PETRELLI · SPOLETO-ROMA

EMME RECLAME · Olivieri

U.S.A./Alitalia, c. 1958

Designer Unknown
Image Courtesy of Swann Auction Galleries

- In this seemingly simple design, an anonymous artist casts the shadows of the Empire State Building and a Douglas DC-7C against the East River, a stately representation of the Manhattan Bridge—complete with filigree detail—serving as the only grounding landmark.

- This is one of the last Alitalia posters to feature a propeller aircraft. In 1958, transatlantic travel changed with the inaugural Boeing 707 Pan Am flight from New York to Paris. With an airspeed of six hundred miles per hour, it was two hundred miles per hour faster than piston-powered airplanes. Alitalia joined the Jet Age two years later with the acquisition of its Douglas DC-8s.

RIGHT

New York/Aer Lingus, c. 1959

Designer Unknown
Private Collection, New York
Image Courtesy of Poster House

- This twilight view of Manhattan seen from under the Brooklyn Bridge shows a perspective that had been popular since the 1930s, when guidebooks such as *King's Views of New York* featured photographs with similar vistas.

- Among the mainly abstract structures within this eye-catching and vividly colored scene are buildings similar to the Cities Service Building, the Bank of Manhattan Trust Building, the City Bank–Farmers Trust Building, and the Irving Trust Company Building.

- The best way to date this poster is through the history of the airline's American service and the different names used to identify the company: Aer Lingus's first transatlantic flight—from Dublin to New York—was on April 28, 1958. The division within Aer Lingus that handled international flights was named Aerlinte Éireann. In 1960, Aerlinte Éireann was renamed Aer Lingus and began describing itself as "Irish international airlines" in 1960.

SABENA/Nach Amerika, 1960

Gaston van den Eynde (1923–83)
Image Courtesy of Poster Connection

- The Société Anonyme Belge d'Exploitation de la Navigation Aérienne (SABENA) was Belgium's national airline from 1923 to 2001. In 1960, it became the first continental European airline to fly jets to the United States.

- This design was originally printed in 1957 with a DC-7C at the upper left; however, once SABENA adopted jets for transatlantic travel, it reissued the poster featuring its new Boeing 707-32.

- Gaston van den Eynde was the director of SABENA's in-house advertising studio, creating numerous posters for the airline with a similar kaleidoscopic

treatment of color. Here, he highlights the view from Roosevelt Island over the East River, with the United Nations, Chrysler, and Empire State Buildings clearly visible.

New York/Go Greyhound, c. 1960

Rod Ruth (1912–87)
Collection of Andrew Zavelson, Chicago
Image Courtesy of Poster House

- This poster promoting bus travel to New York captures a calm, sunny afternoon in the southeast corner of Central Park, where families relax along the edge of the Pond. It is an unexpectedly lyrical and artistic image depicting everyday life in the shadow of the big city.

- Greyhound had its own Art Deco–style bus station in New York City next to the original Pennsylvania Station. When Penn Station was torn down in 1963, the Greyhound terminal followed shortly thereafter. The bus company began to operate out of the current Port Authority Bus Terminal (constructed in 1950) in 1963.

- The "Go Greyhound" slogan was introduced in 1956—ironically, the same year that the Federal-Aid Highway Act went into effect, a thirteen-year program that enhanced and enlarged America's highway system to facilitate long-distance travel by car.

New York/Fly TWA Superjets,
c. 1960

David Klein (1918–2005)
Private Collection, New York
Image Courtesy of Poster House

- In this painting for an unrealized poster, Klein focuses on New York's artistic and cultural heritage, presenting some of the city's most famous statues: the Statue of Liberty; Prometheus in the plaza of Rockefeller Center; George Washington in front of Federal Hall National Memorial on Wall Street; Christopher Columbus at the center of Columbus Circle; and Atlas, the bronze statue by Lee Lawrie, in the courtyard of the International Building of Rockefeller Center.

- In 1960, TWA branded itself the "SuperJet Airline" as part of a new marketing campaign. In March of that year, it began promoting the Boeing 707. While it was not the only airline to operate this aircraft, it got ahead of its competitors by employing creative advertising.

New York/Air-India, 1960

Rustom (Dates Unknown)
Private Collection, New York
Image Courtesy of Poster House

- Part of a larger campaign for Air India, this poster features the airline's famous mascot, the Maharaja. This is the only poster in the series, however, to incorporate photographic elements.

- The Maharaja is always depicted as a rather mischievous character, typically involved in an activity intrinsically connected to the destination being advertised. Here, he is shown riding through the Canyon of Heroes in Manhattan's Financial District in his very own ticker-tape parade.

- The first ticker-tape parade was held in New York in 1886, with an impromptu event marking the dedication of the Statue of Liberty. During the 1920s, they began to be held more regularly and soon became a New York City tradition.

- These parades also became international in scope and celebrated such prominent figures as Theodore Roosevelt, General John Pershing, Charles Lindbergh, Gertrude Ederle (the first woman to swim across the English Channel), and Amelia Earhart, as well as European royalty and international sports stars.

New York/American Airlines, c. 1960. Van Kaufman.

New York/American Airlines, c. 1960

Van Kaufman (1918–95)
Poster House Permanent Collection
Image Courtesy of Poster House

- Similar in style to Galli's poster for United Air Lines (see page 190), this design features an elegant couple emerging from a hansom cab. Here, however, the romantic scene is dominated by the imposing nature of the city at night, the glaring lights of an oncoming car serving as a stark reminder of the reality of the urban environment.

- A widely distributed 1964 postcard features a line of hansom cabs outside the Plaza Hotel. On the verso, it read in part: "unique, in a city noted for progress and speed is the sight of the top-hatted drivers slowly trotting along on their horse-drawn carriages next to sleek and shiny automobiles."

New York/United Air Lines, c. 1961

Stanley Walter Galli (1912–2009)
Image Courtesy of postercorner.com

- Stanley Galli designed some of the most iconic posters for United Air Lines throughout the 1950s and '60s. A painter as well as a commercial artist, he specialized in glamorous portrayals of domestic destinations that would not have been out of place on a Hollywood film set.

- This poster features an imaginary backdrop for the Theater District in Times Square, as can be gleaned by the ladder above the man's head—a common fixture on the sides of theaters.

- While evening gloves were in fashion throughout the 1940s, '50s, and '60s, Audrey Hepburn's famous outfit in the 1961 film *Breakfast at Tiffany*'s made them even more popular.

Swissair/USA, 1961

Nikolaus Schwabe (b. 1926)
*Collection Galerie 1 2 3 -
Geneva/Switzerland
www.galerie123.com*

- In 1961, Nikolaus Schwabe was commissioned to produce a number of posters for Swissair, each representing a different foreign destination. His designs are all based on a collage style and feature identifying symbols of the relevant cities in slightly distorted, out-of-focus compositions.

- As with many posters advertising New York, in this example the city serves as a proxy for all of the United States. While that may seem reductive today, at the time New York was by far the most popular tourist destination in America, with most foreigners only having a vague idea of the country's geography beyond Manhattan.

- In addition to the familiar skyscrapers in the background, Schwabe included the front half of what appears to be a stylized Cadillac. A large vehicle of this kind was a uniquely American symbol at the time, boldly reflecting the country's excess and optimism.

New York/Air-India, 1961

K. K. Save (Dates Unknown)
© *David Pollack Vintage Posters*

- Air India used two versions of this design the same year. In the first—created to promote general travel to India—the central elephant motif is on a bright yellow background, with the Maharaja tossing a ladder down to a woman in a convertible, inviting her to join him.

- Here, the Maharaja sits inside a *houdah* (a canopied seat specifically made for riding on the back of an elephant) elegantly sniffing at a rose. The elephant—a symbol of strength, power, wisdom, and divinity—is bedecked in a patterned *jhool* (saddlecloth). Meanwhile, a *mahout* (trainer) carefully guides the elephant down a busy, highly stylized Manhattan avenue, followed by huge American cars typical of the era, such as the Cadillac Eldorado and the Chevrolet Bel Air. Given the pomp and pageantry associated with this type of scene, visiting New York is presented as on par with a celebration or festival.

New York via UNITED AIR LINES

New York/United Air Lines, c. 1963

Designer Unknown
Image Courtesy of Swann Auction Galleries

- This photographic composition shows a worm's-eye view of Lee Lawrie's famous statue of Atlas watching over the courtyard of the Rockefeller Center complex. This unusual perspective emphasizes the sheer scale of the International

Building that towers behind it, one of the many remarkable structures to be found in New York.

- Installed in 1937, the statue of Atlas was designed in the same Art Deco style as the surrounding architecture. Together, the figure and the celestial orb that he supports are forty-five feet high.

New York/Fly TWA Jets, c. 1963

David Klein (1918–2005)
Private Collection, New York
Image Courtesy of Poster House

- In this painting for an unrealized poster, David Klein combines typography and images in a collaged representation of New York. Many of the featured details do not appear in other compositions by the artist, among them Augustus Saint-Gaudens's General William Tecumseh

Sherman monument in Manhattan's Grand Army Plaza, the iconic lions on the steps of the New York Public Library, the United Nations Secretariat Building, and a street sign and fire call box.

- Most importantly, Klein depicts the TWA Flight Center at JFK Airport, the former of which was designed by Eero Saarinen and Associates and dedicated in May 1962. This celebrated modernist design never actually appeared in any of the airline's extensive poster campaigns.

5TH AVE
MUSIC
Coliseum
LINCOLN CENTER
Park Avenue
OPERA
SHOPS
GALLERIES
Central Park
GRAND CENTRAL STATION
NEW YORK
BROOKLYN
RESTAURANTS
BRONX ZOO
Columbus Circle
CONCERTS
HOTELS
42ND STREET
UNITED NATIONS
HUDSON RIVER
EAST RIVER DRIVE
KENNEDY AIRPORT
WALL ST.
METROPOLITAN MUSEUM
TIMES SQUARE
Shubert Alley
Greenwich Village
BROADWAY
Sutton Place
STATEN ISLAND
Madison Avenue
FLY
TWA
JETS

Fly TWA Jets/New York, c. 1964

David Klein (1918–2005)
Private Collection, New York
Image Courtesy of Poster House

- This painting for an unrealized poster is an exceptional typographic montage of New York City neighborhoods, buildings, locations, and destinations.

- The text radiates from the Statue of Liberty's torch, illuminating the myriad attractions of the great city. The use of words rather than images allows the artist to represent the city's activities and arteries more broadly, referencing such attractions as galleries, restaurants, shops, and the Bronx Zoo, as well as thoroughfares like East River Drive, Madison Avenue, and Park Avenue.

- The inclusion of the name "Kennedy Airport" helps to date the design, as it was known as Idlewild Airport until December 1963.

- Much of the imagery below the typography found its way into a published poster designed by the artist for the city. The Washington Arch is the only notable exclusion.

National Airlines/New York, c. 1964

Bill Simon (Dates Unknown)
Private Collection, NYC
Image Courtesy of Poster House

- National Airlines was a Florida-based carrier that operated from 1934 to 1980, when it was acquired by Pan Am.

- In the 1960s, Bill Simon produced a series of vibrant posters for the airline, many showing uniquely intimate or unusual aspects of a given destination. In this example, a couple is shown enjoying the hospitality at Stouffer's Top of the Sixes, the celebrated rooftop restaurant at 666 Fifth Avenue, against the glamorous backdrop of the Manhattan skyline visible through the plate-glass windows. This restaurant, open between 1958 and 1996, was known not for its food but for its special brand of New York style, and as an ideal place for a graduation celebration or a proposal.

- As a cute Easter egg, the artist included his name on the cover of the pink menu in the lower right corner.

**See Your U.S.A./New York/
Go Greyhound**, c. 1965

Roth (Dates Unknown)
*Image Courtesy of The Ross
Art Group Inc.*

- This unusual composition in the style
  of a rough sketch shows the timeless
  image of a horse-drawn carriage at the
  corner of Grand Army Plaza at Central
  Park. On the right, the stately facade
  of the Metropolitan Club, designed in
  1894 by Stanford White, stands in sharp
  contrast to those of the many high-rises
  near it on Fifth Avenue.

- The poster's designer, known only as
  Roth, created a handful of images for
  Greyhound Lines, each highlighting an
  unexpected glimpse of an American
  city as part of the company's "See Your
  U.S.A." campaign.

- Despite the fact that an overwhelming
  number of New York residents favor the
  abolishment of horse-drawn carriage
  rides in Central Park, they remain
  popular with tourists.

SEE YOUR U.S.A.

NEW YORK

ROTH

GO GREYHOUND ...and leave the driving to us

New York City/Delta Air Lines, c. 1965

Fred Sweney (1912–96)
Image Courtesy of antiqueposters.com

- In the 1960s, Delta commissioned Fred Sweney to create a series of posters promoting various domestic destinations, each highlighting notable sites in the respective cities.

- Here, Sweney presents a collection of New York landmarks, including the United Nations complex; Rockefeller Center's Prometheus statue, its row of international flags, and the fountains of the Channel Gardens; the Empire State Building; the Statue of Liberty; and the Guggenheim Museum.

- Sweney was an illustrator, painter, and author of several art-instruction books, including *The Art of Painting and Drawing Animals*. Between 1950 and 1976, he taught graphic design at what was then known as the Ringling School of Art (now the Ringling College of Art and Design) in Sarasota, Florida.

New York/Air-India, 1966

Art Director: J.B. Cowashi
(Dates Unknown)
Illustrator: S.N. Surti (Dates Unknown)
© David Pollack Vintage Posters

- Air India's mischievous mascot, the
  Maharaja, featured in many of the
  airline's posters. Here, he has taken

on the guises of various international
delegates to the United Nations as they
parade in front of its famous buildings.

- The pink color reflected on the General
  Assembly Building in the foreground indicates an evening scene, the delegates
  leaving after a long day of negotiations
  to make the world a safer place.

- The United Nations complex, in particular
  the Secretariat Building, became a New
  York landmark in 1952—the same year
  that it was both completed and occupied.
  Its International Style mirrored the aims
  of the organization it housed.

New York/Alitalia, 1966

Hartmut Hielscher (1942–96)
Image Courtesy of Poster Connection

- During the 1960s, Hartmut Hielscher designed a series of posters for Alitalia, all of which incorporated clippings from magazines and newspapers local to the destinations advertised. From a distance, these wonderfully detailed collages seem to show the notable landmarks in each location—in this instance, the iconic skyline of New York City.

- Here, cuttings from *LIFE* magazine, the *New York Herald Tribune*, and the *New York Times*, among other regional publications and brand names, effectively describe the city in which they are based.

NEW YORK

ALITALIA

NEW YORK

DELTA AIR LINES

ABOVE

New York/Delta Air Lines, 1967

John Hardy (1923–2004)
By Potter and Potter Auctions/Gado

- John Hardy produced numerous posters for Delta Air Lines in the late 1960s, most of which feature an individual character associated with a given destination. For New York City, he focuses on an NYPD officer blowing a whistle at the intersection of Forty-Second Street and Broadway in Times Square.

- The poster also features a Douglas DC-8-61 on the right, a plane that Delta started flying in 1967. DC-8-61s were effectively stretched DC-8s, with the largest seat capacity of any aircraft until the advent of the Boeing 747 in 1970.

OPPOSITE

Discover North America/SAS, 1968

Jørn Freddie (1929–2008)
Image Courtesy of Illustration Gallery

- Jørn Freddie was a Danish photographer, primarily known for his work in fashion. This is one of his few commercial posters.

- This unexpected worm's-eye view of the Avenue of the Americas (commonly known as Sixth Avenue) captures the overwhelming sensation of encountering "skyscraper alley," which includes

upshot depictions of the towers of Rockefeller Center West. Eero Saarinen's iconic CBS tower, known as Black Rock, is partly visible at the lower right. Most of the corporate headquarters in Midtown are glass slabs built in the International Style.

- Scandinavian Airlines (SAS) is the flag carrier of Denmark, Norway, and Sweden. In 1968, like other European airlines, the carrier wanted to encourage travel to the United States as part of a larger agreement with the US government to help offset a $2 billion tourism deficit between the US and the rest of the world, primarily Europe.

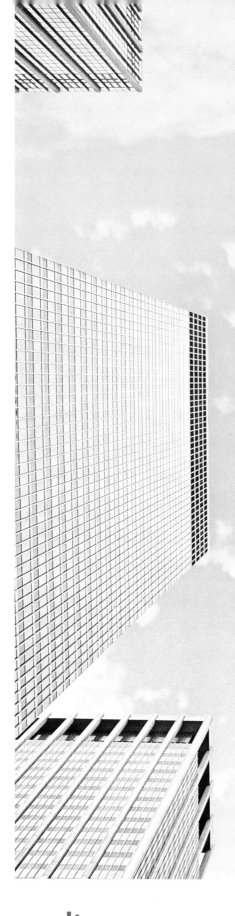

Avenue of the Americas, New York

discover
NORTH AMERICA

SAS *SCANDINAVIAN AIRLINES*

Harlem, 1968

Peter Teubner (b. 1935)
Poster House Permanent Collection
Image Courtesy of Poster House

- In a clever integration of the letter *H*, Peter Teubner captures the liveliness of Harlem's 125th Street in fluorescent pink, including the neon marquee of the Apollo Theater and an electric symphony of traffic and streetlights.

- Although not a travel poster, this is one in a series of ten images called "Aspects of New York City" designed on behalf of the Container Corporation of America by various artists. The posters were hung in public places around the city to celebrate its beauty and diversity.

- In spite of Harlem's international renown, very few posters promote it, making this a particularly significant design.

- The Container Corporation of America manufactured humble corrugated cardboard boxes but from its founding in 1928, its advertising always featured the latest in graphic design.

65 Bridges to New York, 1968

Tomoko Miho (1931–2012)
Poster House Permanent Collection
Image Courtesy of Poster House

- This is one of four posters created by the Japanese American designer Tomoko Miho for the Container Corporation of America's "Aspects of New York City" series. It shows a nearly abstract close-up of the Verrazzano-Narrows Bridge shrouded in fog.

- As a child, Miho spent three years in an internment camp in Arizona with her family. Later, she designed catalogs for Herman Miller, the American furniture company known for its modernist aesthetic.

- Since the Department of Transportation lists 803 bridges within New York City that fall under its purview, it is not possible to identify the 65 bridges referenced by Miho.

65 bridges   to new york

wall st

Wall St, 1968

Tomoko Miho (1931–2012)
Poster House Permanent Collection
Image Courtesy of Poster House

- To represent Wall Street here, Tomoko Miho combined architecture and finance, creating the skyscrapers from blocks of glass and printed stock-price listings.

- Miho's work champions both modernism and minimalism and was largely influenced by the Swiss International Style, which she learned about on a months-long trip to Europe in 1960. There, she met prominent designers Giovanni Pintori, Hans Erni, Herbert Leupin, and Ristomatti Ratia.

American Airlines/New York, 1971

Harry Bertschmann (b. 1931)
Image Courtesy of The Ross Art Group Inc.

- American Airlines's "Endless Summer" campaign was launched in April 1971, with a series of brightly colored posters created by various designers. Named after the 1966 cult movie about young surfers traveling the world on commercial airlines in search of the "perfect wave," the series was intended to capture a specific moment in pop culture and attract the youth market.

- Although many of the images focus on exotic destinations like Acapulco and Haiti, with his bright color palette and whimsical waterfront scene, Harry Bertschmann transforms the concrete-and-glass cityscape of New York City into a tropical paradise.

- Visible in the upper left are the Twin Towers under construction, including the kangaroo cranes located on the South Tower—so named because they could automatically move up from one floor to the next (in addition to the fact that they were made in Australia).

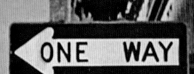

Lufthansa/New York, 1972

Designer Unknown
Image Courtesy of Galerie 1881, Paris

- This photographic poster presents a view up Fifth Avenue from Seventeenth Street toward the Empire State Building. Rather than highlighting a popular destination, it captures an unlikely and picturesque vignette of the city, then entering one of its grittiest decades. The foreground of the image is dominated by one of the original Edison Illuminating Company's cast-iron twin-lamp lampposts, the first of which were installed

on this stretch of Fifth Avenue in 1892. Very few of them survive today.

- In 1969, Otto "Otl" Aicher (best known for overseeing the design for the 1972 Munich Olympics) reworked Lufthansa's corporate identity. He stressed the importance of photography to promote modernity, presenting clear guidelines for its use.

- While Aicher made many photographs specifically for Lufthansa's advertising programs, most were taken by Erwin Fieger and Hans Hansen. It is not clear which of the three took the photograph used in this poster.

New York/Southern, c. 1975

Designer Unknown
Image Courtesy of Poster Connection

- Southern Airways was a regional airline, focusing on transportation between small cities and major destinations within the country. It typically operated multi-stop routes rather than one-stop direct flights. This poster promotes a three-leg journey beginning in Columbus, Georgia, stopping in Washington, DC, and then traveling on to New York City.

- All the posters for Southern Airways from this period feature saturated colors and a large DC-9 aircraft flying over points

of interest at the relevant destination. In this case, the newly opened Twin Towers join the Statue of Liberty, the Brooklyn Bridge, and the lights of Broadway against a skyline that provides a glimpse of the Empire State Building. Not all of Southern's destinations were associated with such history and glamour—its Milwaukee poster, for example, features a cow and two fishermen.

- Although the designer of the poster series is unknown, the logo was created in 1973 by Wolfgang Rekow of Lee & Young Communications. In 1979, the airline merged with North Central Airlines, becoming Republic Airlines.

New York/United Airlines,
c. 1975

R. Meyer (Dates Unknown)
Image Courtesy of Illustration Gallery

- This poster shows a south-facing view within Central Park, focusing on Gapstow Bridge, which crosses the northeast end of the Pond. The famous Plaza Hotel, the new structure at 9 West Fifty-Seventh Street (famous for its giant red 9 sculpture on the sidewalk in front of it), and the top of the Park Lane hotel are visible in the background.

- The composition also reflects Saul Bass's new visual identity for United Air Lines, introduced in 1974. The rebranding featured the distinctive "flying U" symbol. An orange stripe was also added to the logo to supply warmth and distinguish United's colors from the standard red, white, and blue of many other airlines. Finally, the company's name was changed from United Air Lines to United Airlines.

Saul Steinberg, *View of the World from 9th Avenue*

Cover of *The New Yorker*,
March 29, 1976
*© The Saul Steinberg Foundation/
Artists Rights Society (ARS), New York
Cover reprinted with permission of
The New Yorker magazine. All rights
reserved.*

IMAGE COURTESY OF SWANN AUCTION GALLERIES

- Of the ninety covers that Saul Steinberg (1914–99) produced for *The New Yorker* magazine, this one became by far the most famous, so much so that the publication soon reissued it as a promotional poster.

- Steinberg's tongue-in-cheek presentation of New York City as not just the fulcrum of the United States but of the entire world, was a fair reflection of how some of the city's residents saw their home, even during a decade when it was marked by extreme economic and social turmoil.

- In the patchwork quilt of old Manhattan neighborhoods, Hell's Kitchen—between Thirty-Fourth and Fiftieth Streets and west of Eighth Avenue—was one of the last to become gentrified. As such, Steinberg's choice to make it the center of the world in this image is quite curious.

The New Yorker, 1979

The New Yorker, 1979

R.O. Blechman (b. 1930)
*Poster Photo Archives, Posters Please,
Inc., NYC*

- In his spare and refined depiction of
Manhattan, R.O. Blechman outlines some
of the city's landmark structures with his
trademark black ink, accentuating them
with glowing spires and facades.

- This selective coloring allows him to
highlight the Forty-Sixth Street elevation

of the New York Central Building, the
Empire State Building, and the Chrysler
Building, as well as other ubiquitous but
less celebrated features of the city, like
its cedar water towers.

- Between 1974 and 1996, Blechman
produced fifteen covers for *The New
Yorker*, but this was the only one that
was enlarged as an advertisement.
He has won awards for his work as a
cartoonist, film director, and advertising designer. In 1973, the Museum
of Modern Art in New York presented a
retrospective of his work.

The New Yorker, 1979

Oanh Pham-Phu (b. 1939)
*Poster Photo Archives, Posters Please,
Inc., NYC*

- Oanh Pham-Phu was born in Saigon
during the Japanese occupation. He
has also been a resident of the United
States, Japan, Germany, and Hungary,
and his work therefore has a truly international perspective.

- This design started as a cover for *The
New Yorker* but was enlarged that year
as an advertising poster. In it, Pham-Phu
highlights the international binary
language of computer punch cards,
represented as pastel-tinted skyscrapers
in the classic Manhattan skyline.

- The cards shown in this composition
were modeled on those introduced
by IBM in 1928. By 1979, the year this
poster was designed, they were generally being replaced by magnetic tape,
which was rather less attractive.

American Airlines / New York

OPPOSITE

Pan Am/New York, 1980

Designer Unknown
*Image Courtesy of Potter
& Potter Auctions*

- In 1970, Pan American hired the New York design firm of Chermayeff & Geismar to revitalize its brand identity. One of its first suggestions was that the airline should embrace the fact that most people simply referred to it as Pan Am. This was the first series of advertisements that incorporated the new, abbreviated name.

- Unlike most air-travel posters, this one highlights neither an airplane nor a destination, but instead shows the airline's

new headquarters, designed by renowned architect Walter Gropius. This structure, at Park Avenue and Forty-Fifth Street, with "PAN AM" emblazoned across the top of its facade, instantly became the most famous airline headquarters in the country, if not the world. When it was completed in 1963, it also became the world's largest office building.

- As part of the project, Ivan Chermayeff designed a series of twelve posters featuring photographic images of remote destinations. It was seen as so important to the history of graphic design that the entire set was acquired by the Museum of Modern Art in 1972. While this poster is not part of that original set, subsequent designers attempted to mimic it in their work for Pan Am.

ABOVE

American Airlines/New York,
c. 1980

Designer Unknown
*Poster Photo Archives, Posters Please,
Inc., NYC*

- This photographic composition presents a view of Lower Manhattan as seen from Brooklyn. The dramatic arch of the Brooklyn Bridge partially obscures the illuminated Twin Towers at the center, while 40 Wall Street (formerly the Manhattan Company Building) and 70 Pine Street (originally the Cities Service Building) are visible on the far left.

- The bridge, designated a National Historic Civil Engineering Landmark in 1972, continues to fulfill the dual roles of destination in its own right and public thoroughfare. By 1980, however, the bridge was in dire condition and faced closure.

- Between 1980 and 1983, the city funded a $153 million program to renovate it in advance of its centenary celebrations on May 24, 1983. The event attracted a reported 650,000 revelers to the Brooklyn waterfront and another 1.5 million to the opposite side of the East River. Ed Koch, the mayor at the time, declared, "The bridge is the unification of the city. With the bridge we became a single city."

New York/Piedmont, c. 1984

Designer Unknown
*Poster Photo Archives, Posters Please,
Inc., NYC*

- The designer of this striking image has focused on the Art Deco crown of the Chrysler Building glowing at sunset rather than on the Manhattan skyline as a whole. This ambitious structure, once the tallest in the world, represents Piedmont as "The Up-and-Coming Airline."

- Ironically, the brownish-copper haze, possibly intended to appear romantic, actually points to the pollution problems that the city faced at the time—although by the mid-1980s, they were past their worst. When New York City was struck by wildfire smoke in the summer of 2023, the air quality was described as back at levels "not seen since the 1980s."

- After various mergers, Piedmont Airlines is now a regional airline operating as an American Eagle carrier. It no longer serves New York City.

NEW YORK

END OF AN ERA

The number of visitors to New York City drastically declined after the events of September 11, 2001, when the Twin Towers of the World Trade Center were attacked by terrorists who had hijacked four planes, two of which were targeted at New York City. It took almost five years for New York tourism to reach its pre-9/11 level—but the date of the attacks marks an effective end to the proliferation of poster designs intended to lure travelers to the city. Since then, an increased reliance on the internet and social media has mitigated the need for "old-fashioned" printed advertising, and, as a result, hardly any notable posters promoting travel to New York City have been published.

The skyline continues to change, evolve, and grow ever higher—One World Trade Center is now the tallest building in the United States, and five other buildings have been constructed throughout Manhattan, each taller than the Empire State Building. Yet none these structures, nor the new silhouette of the city, have appeared in travel posters. The genius of construction and marvels of engineering continue to define the city's appearance, but these new buildings, in all their glory, have failed to capture the imagination of the world in the same way as the original Twin Towers. While people turn to their mobile devices for inspiration and information on travel, the placards that enthralled previous generations become all the more scintillating and elusive.

OPPOSITE

Pan Am/USA, c. 1973

Designer Unknown
Poster Photo Archives, Posters Please, Inc., NYC

In the 1970s, posters, especially those promoting travel, gradually moved away from illustration toward photography. Of the airlines, Pan Am seemed to lead the way in this trend, quickly adapting dramatic, "real" imagery of its numerous destinations to its advertising campaigns.

When the World Trade Center was completed in 1973, it instantly became a landmark in the New York City skyline. The sheer size of its Twin Towers created a powerful juxtaposition with the city's first advertising icon, the Statue of Liberty, inspiring many photographers to capture these structures together from the water. At the time, the World Trade Center reflected the general optimism of the 1960s, when the buildings were conceived, rather than the gloom surrounding the harsh economic reality of the 1970s.

New York/Continental Airlines, c. 1973

Designer Unknown
Image Courtesy of Etsy

- In 1967, Continental Airlines introduced a new color scheme and logo designed by Saul Bass, both of which are featured in this poster. The brand's new livery consisted of orange, red, and gold colors.

- Meanwhile, the logo was transformed from a stylized eagle to the contrails motif of a circle bisected by fanning air routes. The symbol was intended to suggest the powerful thrust of the jet engine combined with the airflow patterns of high-speed flight, but it became popularly known as "the meatball."

- While the distance between the Statue of Liberty and the Twin Towers was actually 2.2 miles, this photograph establishes a dramatically foreshortened perspective, making the landmarks appear to be adjacent.

- This kind of comparison between the Statue of Liberty and the Twin Towers represented more than serendipitous proximity. When they opened, each was the tallest structure in New York at the time. An image of the statue dwarfed by the towers served to underscore both the real and the metaphoric growth of the city over the intervening decades.

New York/Pan Am, c. 1975

Designer Unknown
Image Courtesy of Swann Auction Galleries

- In addition to the juxtaposition of the Twin Towers with the Statue of Liberty frequently deployed by the airlines, Pan Am was among those that also incorporated images of the Brooklyn Bridge into their advertisements for travel to New York City. An engineering marvel in its day, the bridge was completed in 1883 and stands as one of the city's most recognizable landmarks. Until the completion of the Statue of Liberty in 1886, the Brooklyn Bridge was also the tallest structure in the city.

- To construct the bridge, pneumatic caissons (large, watertight structures filled with compressed air) were used, allowing for underwater excavation. When the construction teams hit bedrock, the caissons were filled with concrete to complete the foundations. The caisson on the Brooklyn side of the bridge sits forty-four feet below the water, while the one on the Manhattan side rests seventy-eight feet below it.

- As with the Brooklyn Bridge, the setting of the foundations for the World Trade Center was a challenge, especially given that the building site had once been submerged below the Hudson River. Crews dug seventy feet below the surface in order to hit bedrock before building a perimeter wall (known as a slurry wall) to hold back groundwater. This "bathtub" then allowed the rest of the excavation and construction to proceed.

NEW YORK

New York

TWA

Trans World Airlines/New York, c. 1976

Designer Unknown
Poster House Permanent Collection
Image Courtesy of Poster House

- Erected between 1966 and 1973, the World Trade Center was a complex of seven buildings located in the Financial District of Lower Manhattan. From the time of their construction, the 110-story Twin Towers became a defining feature of the New York City skyline.

- This poster shows how the towers dwarfed the surrounding architectural landscape, and points to the evolution of the Financial District by including the old and the new side by side.

- While the poster is undated, it had to be printed prior to the installation of an enormous antenna on top of North Tower in 1979.

- The most curious aspect of this design is the unexpected use of the Peignot typeface to spell out New York. Designed by A. M. Cassandre in 1937, it does not have a lower case. In this instance, the letters roughly emulate the jagged skyline, with some extending higher than others.

RIGHT

Lufthansa, c. 1985

Designer Unknown
Poster Photo Archives, Posters Please,
Inc., NYC

- More than two hundred thousand tons of steel were used to construct the Twin Towers. Because of their remarkable height, the towers were engineered to sway up to three feet in any direction on a windy day.

- The buildings also incorporated a radical, framed-tube structure that provided strength without the need for internal columns. This allowed for more interior space, but it also meant that the windows had to be narrower than on other skyscrapers. This did not pose a problem for the architect, Minoru Yamasaki, who was afraid of heights and therefore wanted windows that were narrower than his shoulders to impart a feeling of security.

- Windows on the World, the famed restaurant on the 106th and 107th floors of the North Tower, was the best place in Manhattan to see New York at night, and very shortly after it opened in 1976, it had a six-month waiting list for reservations. Noted designer Milton Glaser was hired to create the menu artwork and the dishware patterns.

New York

△DELTA AIR LINES

some of the most famous welcoming symbols of New York City.

• The Woolworth Building of 1913 is also visible in the background of this poster; like the World Trade Center, it featured neo-Gothic motifs and was the tallest building in the world at the time of its construction.

• This poster provides one of the most realistic views of the Twin Towers since their extreme height meant that they were often at least partially obscured by fog, mist, or clouds.

• After enduring three bankruptcies, TWA was sold to American Airlines in 2001—two years after this poster was published. Rather than keep the airline afloat as a separate entity, it was subsumed by the larger company.

• That same year, the Twin Towers—displayed prominently here on the right—were also destroyed, making this poster one of the last advertisements to include both the brand and the buildings.

• This photograph was most likely taken from DUMBO in Brooklyn, documenting the Twin Towers, the Brooklyn Bridge, and a sliver of the Empire State Building.

NEW YORK

TWA®

ABOUT POSTER HOUSE

BY JULIA KNIGHT
DIRECTOR OF POSTER HOUSE

When Poster House opened in Manhattan in June of 2019, it was the first and only museum in the United States dedicated to the global history of posters, covering their design, impact, and storytelling ability.

In a city full of long-established museums and arts nonprofits, we truly believed there was room in the landscape for an institution that would use everyday material culture to illuminate history and help understand our complex relationship with visual literacy. Everyone has a poster story—people either grew up with them, collect them, have a favorite, or have memories of ones that made an impact. It's a medium that everyone can innately relate to and understand.

Since posters were meant to be temporary documents, they also encourage experimentation, time-specific design, and can be linked with niche movements that bring the past to life, which is especially meaningful in a time where there is great pressure to reconsider and revise history. Poster House wishes to provide a place to engage with and understand that history without sanitizing or glorifying it.

Posters are intended for everyone and designed for engagement, and Poster House applies those values to all our programming, exhibitions, and particularly our texts. The goal of every museum project is to connect audiences with fascinating information in as clear and concise a way as the posters themselves, and we have brought that ethos to this book as well.

For our five-year anniversary in 2024, Poster House is hosting *Wonder City of the World: New York City Travel Posters*, an original exhibition chronicling how our city was promoted from the late 1800s through the 1980s with posters. This show is a love letter to New York, the place that supported us in our early years of development and where we found our first devoted audience—and we are thrilled to present a subject that will forever hold value for the poster fans and Big Apple enthusiasts among us. The exhibition will tell the story of how New York grew from a gateway to idyllic upstate resorts to one of the largest tourist destinations in the world—and this catalog expands on the confines of that show and allows us to look at even more posters and their spectacular designs over the ensuing decades.

We are grateful that Abrams approached us to work on this book, our first exhibition catalog published in tandem with a Poster House project. We hope it is the foundation for many more to come.

WONDER CITY OF THE WORLD

NEW YORK CITY

TRAVEL POSTERS

ISBN: 978-1-4197-7409-6
Library of Congress CIP data is available
© 2024 Poster House
Printed and Bound in Hong Kong
10 9 8 7 6 5 4 3 2 1
Cernunnos logo design: Mark Ryden
Book design: Benjamin Brard

Abrams books are available at special discounts when purchased in quantity
for premiums and promotions as well as fundraising or educational use.
Special editions can also be created to specification. For details, contact
specialsales@abramsbooks.com or the address below.

ABRAMS The Art of Books
195 Broadway, New York, NY 10007
abramsbooks.com